The Art of Falling in Love with Your Enemy

ANNE KEMP

Copyright © 2023 by Anne Kemp

All rights reserved.

No part of this book may be reproduced in any form or by any electronic or mechanical means, including information storage and retrieval systems, without written permission from the author, except for the use of brief quotations in a book review.

For Brett and Liz
Two of the strongest people I know.
Anne xo

ONE
Zac

Looking down at the tiny schnauzer sprawled across my feet, I shake my head. I'm not sure how many police stations in the state of North Carolina have fans, but ours seem to come as the four-legged kind. This particular fella appeared at the station for the first time about a week after I started working here, at the Sweetkiss Creek Police department. He's cute, and really lovable, but he's not supposed to be here.

Bending down, I scratch Thor's sweet spot, that little patch of fur between his ears. I'm mesmerized when he closes his eyes, completely relaxing into my hand. So trusting.

"He's back?" Sergeant Lane asks as he pauses in front of me, taking the time to peer over my desk and get a look at Thor. "I swear if he comes in one more time, he's coming with me for my kids. They'll love him."

Glancing down at my feet, I find my friend with one eye open, watching me. Thor's big brown eyes are not that dissimilar to a baby deer's, and their depth is infinite. He's not just a dog when he looks at me...it's like he sees through me.

It takes me less than a millisecond to scoop the little guy

up from the floor and into my arms so I can snuggle him close. "He's obviously smitten, so if anyone gets to take him home at any point, it's gonna be me."

"Well, we both know who the owner is," Lane says out of the side of his mouth, chewing back a grin. "Are you gonna tell her he's here again, or do I have the distinct pleasure?"

Sighing, I run my fingers through Thor's fur, combing it down on the crown of his head at the same time he slams his body against mine and fully melts into my chest. As much as I want to keep him, I know what I have to do. Flipping the bone-shaped tag over that dangles from his collar, I see the digits I need to dial to tell his owner he's here. I quickly punch in the numbers, but I'm sent to voicemail immediately, leaving me to wonder if the universe is trying to tell me to keep the dog. When I try calling again and get the same result, I cover my bases this time: I leave a message before hanging up and sending a quick text to Thor's owner.

My job is now done, so I commence with cuddles. There's nothing wrong with a grown man in his police uniform cuddling a small schnauzer against his chest, is there?

However, the sound of someone clearing their throat behind me takes me out my sugary-sweet schnauzer-trance.

"Is this your newest girlfriend? Mom and Dad are gonna be surprised."

I turn around, finding my younger brother, Tuck, standing in front of me, dressed to the nines. "That's a serious suit you're wearing."

"I'm a serious guy," he says with a wink before pulling me into a big hug, albeit an awkward one since Thor won't move from my arms. "Can a guy stop in to say hi to his big brother?"

"As long as you're not speeding on your way to do it, sure." Looking Tuck up and down, I have to admit he does look like he's a proper businessman, an executive even. I know my mom would be so proud that at least one member of our family decided to follow in her footsteps and work as a lawyer. "So what are you up to today? Chasing ambulances?"

"Ha." Tuck punches me in the arm, eliciting a growl from Thor. He holds his hands up in the air, eyes wide. "Ayyy. Sorry, little guy." Tuck's green eyes flash when he looks at me. "Who is this and where does it belong?"

"This would be Thor, and he belongs to one of our sweet, local residents here in Sweetkiss Creek." My lips torque at the end of that sentence instead of spreading into a smile, thanks to a rogue memory picking this very moment in time to pop up.

Thor belongs to Etta, and Etta and I were kind of set up to go on a double date, to an Escape Room of all things, by our friends Reid and Dylan. It's worth noting that after this double date—not that I would call it that by any means—Reid and Dylan realized they had feelings for each other, and now they're on their road to happily ever after. But me and Etta? Let's just say a line was drawn in the sand that night, and now we try to stay out of each other's way. At least I know I do my best to get out of hers.

The look on Tuck's face tells me that my words have flowed out of my mouth about as sarcastically as I hoped they would. "Well, good thing you're not trying to sell me something because, wow. That was the most insincere description of a person I've ever heard."

"If only you knew." Shrugging my shoulders, I turn my attention back to my lap dog. "If you hang out long enough, you may get to meet Thor's mom. Etta's a treat," I say with an exaggerated chuckle.

"You build her up so well, and while I'd love to hang out and meet little miss sunshine, I need to get on the road so I make my meeting on time. I had to see you since I was literally driving right by here."

"Will you come back this way after your meeting?"

Tuck gives me a clipped nod. "Yep. I'll be back this way tomorrow, probably late afternoon. I was hoping I could stay the night? Bethany is in full renovation mode at the house and our master bedroom has been taken over."

Knowing how much Tuck loves his quiet time, I can only grin. "Is it making you crazy?"

Indifference bounces his shoulder. "Eh. She's worth it. I trust Bethany not to stick us with lace, pinks, or other pastel colors that might make me crazy." Tuck exhales, rolling his eyes. "Laney has been helping us, too, and that's been awesome. We both really enjoy having her around."

My thoughts flash to our sister, Laney, who's back in Beaufort working at the fire department there. She followed in my dad's footsteps and decided to be a career firefighter. Tuck, as mentioned, is a lawyer, and me...well, I decided I wanted to be a police officer just to round out the whole public-servant-family thing.

"Well, see, there's a positive. Renovations bring families together." Winking, I slug his arm. "Should put that on a coffee mug."

"I'd like to hit you with that coffee mug." Tuck, with a glint in his eye, indicates toward the front of the station. "Race me to my car?"

There's only a two-year age difference between us, so saying we're competitive is kind of a joke. We're over-the-top in an at each other's throats kind of competitive, yet loving, way that only brothers can be.

Which means, for us, we take every moment we can and make it a competition.

"I can't race you, Tuck. I'm at work and we're adults."

Tuck rolls his eyes. "C'mon. I saw a coffee cart outside, serving homemade apple fritters. Loser buys coffee and fritters?"

I'm a weak man, what can I say? I glance around the station, which is oddly empty except for Kenny who's been shopping online all day. And I'm holding a dog. Can I run with this animal? I look back at Tuck and start to shake my head no in an effort to throw him off course, then I slap his back and take off at a full sprint.

"Let's do it!" I call out over my shoulder as I clear the lobby and throw open the outside door.

Do we tear out of the station like grown men who shouldn't be racing? Why, yes, we do. Do I manage to almost run over Lane? Why, yes, I do. Am I holding on to Thor precariously as I do all of this, like a juggler attempting to keep his balls in the air? I'm sure I do.

But the real question is...do I make it to his car first in the parking lot?

No, I don't.

Tuck, always the faster of the two of us, slips past me and slams his hand on the hood of his car as I slam into it at full speed, breathing heavily. Still clutching Thor, whose tongue lolls about out of the side of his mouth in giddy happiness, I catch my breath and turn to face Tuck, finding him with a sneer spread across his lips.

"I'd like a large coffee...no, scratch that. I'd like a large mocha with extra whipped cream and two apple fritters." He smirks, inclining his head to the cart while he holds his hands out for Thor. "Give me the dog. Off with you."

Laughing, I do as I'm told. It's always been like this. Family game nights over the years were out of control, to the point our parents realized at a young age it would be best for their two boys to be on the same team. Putting our powers together to fight for good, instead of allowing them to clash behind the scenes, meant a quieter life for all involved. But we were still boys who shared a room and did everything together.

I get our order and saunter back over, handing him the

goods as he gets behind the steering wheel, still grinning and holding Thor on his lap.

"Thanks for the pick-me-up for the drive." He toasts the air with his drink. "Tomorrow, we race for our dinner."

"You're actually insane," I manage to say with a laugh. "I forgot to ask if you and Bethany are gonna come with Mom and Dad for the charity fundraiser in a few weeks?"

The Sweetkiss Creek Police Department holds a fundraising event every year to raise money for their department projects. This year they decided to throw a charity ball, allowing the good folks in the area to get out their very best formal dresses and dust off their tuxedos. It's the kind of event that makes me cringe, but I know my parents would want to show up and support the cause because that's how they roll.

"Laney can't get off work, but the rest of us are coming." Taking a bite of his fritter, he eyes me as he chews. In his lap, Thor's nose wiggles in an attempt to sniff at the sugary treasure. I hope that dog licks his food.

Tuck swallows his bite before narrowing his eyes and sizing me up. "Are you bringing a date?"

I can't shake my head no hard enough. "Nah, not in the cards for me right now."

"You can't lick your wounds forever, Zac." Tuck gives me a brotherly look of affection that only a sibling can get away with. "Hearts break, but they get put back together, too."

I know he's right, but when you've been dumped by your college girlfriend for your best friend, well, that's a sting that stays. I just keep hoping someone or something will take its place because I'm ready for that feeling of hopelessness that's lingered since then to be erased.

I start to open my mouth, to thank him for his brotherly words of wisdom, but my cell phone chooses that moment to go off in my back pocket. Shifting my weight from one foot to the other, I swipe my mobile from its hiding spot to peek at the screen. Yep, it's exactly who and what I thought it was.

"I gotta go, Tuck." I put my drink and apple fritter on the roof of his car before leaning in the window to take Thor back. Gathering my things, I incline my head toward the station. "We've got a severe weather event on its way through town at the moment, and you'll be safer if you stay in your car and get to where you're going. And fast."

"Seriously?" Tuck's eyes almost bug out of his head as he sticks his face out the window, craning his neck to look around, and points to Main Street. "It's sunny and still, the perfect fall day. What storm are you even talking about?"

"Oh, there's a storm a-coming." I nod knowingly, petting Thor as I walk backwards, returning to what I hope is the safety of my desk. "Hurricane Etta. This is one storm that is not to be messed with. She pretty much takes out everyone in a two-mile radius when she makes landfall, so you'd better scoot."

"Fine, I'm leaving you, weirdo." Tuck laughs, leaning forward and turning the key in his ignition, bringing the car's engine to life. "I'll text you tomorrow when I'm leaving Asheville and on my way back."

With a wave, he's gone.

Leaving me alone to go back inside and wait for Hurricane Etta to make landfall.

TWO
Etta

Marching up the front steps to the police station, I make sure to keep my head held high and my shoulders back. I swing the main door open—probably a little bit too hard judging by the way it slams against the brick exterior wall—but hey, I'm a girl who likes to make an entrance.

Scanning the lobby, I look around for the officer in charge—or at least the insufferable one who texted me not even an hour ago.

Standing by an old metal desk on the other side of the room, I spot Zac Wright holding Thor tight in his arms. He throws his head back, laughing at something the other officer sitting there is saying.

Who is he to be so light and joyful while holding *my* dog?

It takes me only a few strides to cross the room and land in front of Zac. Crossing my arms in front of my chest, I stare at the furry ball in his arms. Traitor. If I could scold this dog with my eyes, I would, but it'll have to wait until we're in the car. Not that he'll understand, because we know he won't. In fact, I'm willing to bet twenty bucks and a really nice five-star dinner out that he'll do it again later this week.

Dragging my eyes from Thor, they travel upward until slamming into Zac's. Zac and his bright green eyes, sparkling in the sunshine like he's a vampire from those old *Twilight* movies. I'd be bothered by this picture of the perfect man in front of me if he wasn't a pain in my derriere already.

"So." I hold my hands out to take Thor back. "Looks like I need to apologize. Again."

"It's the third time this week, Etta." A devilish smirk curls his lips as he slowly runs his fingers through Thor's fur. "I'm beginning to think that you're sending him here on purpose. Maybe you should start tying notes around his neck for me."

"Do you really think I want to spend my time coming to the police station every day to pick up my dog?" I reach over and gently take Thor out of Zac's arms, pulling the little guy close to my body. His big brown eyes meet mine, and somewhere deep in there I swear an apology swirls. Usually his pathetic little side-eye can get me. Cracks me and makes me forget his bad deeds. Ha. Not today, Thor.

"I have not one clue what it is you want to spend your time doing daily, Etta McCoy. Last I checked, you do not come with an owner's manual." He walks around and pulls the chair out from under his desk. Lowering himself to the chair, he scoots in and moves some paperwork around, smiling at me smugly as he does so. "Now, if you'll excuse me, I am very, very busy."

A quick glance around the office tells me that one thing Zac is not, is busy. The other officer he shares a desk with, Kenny, has his computer open and appears to be shopping online for a new lawnmower. Two other officers I recognize but don't know sit quietly at their desks tapping away on keyboards, and, because his office has windows for walls, I can see Sergeant Lane pacing his space while he's on a phone call.

"I see. It's all hands on deck here today, huh?" Bending over, I place Thor down on the ground and clip his leash to his collar. "Wow. We'd better get out of the way and fast, before you have to do something crazy like...make a pot of coffee."

Zac rolls his eyes and pushes himself away from the desk, taking his time to cross his arms in front of his chest as he cocks his head to one side and glowers in my direction.

"You came, you got your dog, now..." He flicks his hand toward the main door. "Show yourself out. Come again."

"You know, my tax dollars pay your salary, sir. You need to be nice to me."

"I really don't think that's true," Zac manages to say through a skewed grin. Ugh. I hate that grin. I hate that smirky, sexy, lopsided grin with all of my heart and I want to wipe it off his really handsome face. But, I have enough on my plate today without getting held up here. Glancing at my watch, a rush of cold fluid races through my veins. I've got less than twenty minutes to get back home and log in online for my meeting with my lawyer.

"Well, I'd debate this further, but I have to go." Spinning on my heel, I make my way back through the obstacle course they call an office, stopping as I get to the door, and turning around with some added flair...because, hello. We all need a little drama.

"Oh, and Zac?"

Hopeful green eyes flash my way as Zac looks up at me expectantly.

"Stop luring my dog off my property, will ya? You smell like dog treats."

"How is it that he is able to sue me over this?" If I could dramatically fling myself off a cliff right now, I would. "The fact we divorced isn't good enough, now he's got to come for me over the rights to the winery?"

"I know it's a tough situation, but he doesn't have a leg to stand on. You can rest easy with that." Alex Miller, my lawyer based in Washington D.C., is way more optimistic about this situation than I am.

"Tough situation? We had an agreement. He got what we created during our marriage. During. For the duration of. Logos, marketing, wines...all that jazz he came up with, with me in our brainstorming meetings, at the time of our marriage. It wasn't much that he helped with, if we're being honest, so I feel even acknowledgement of that was quite generous on my part. However, the idea for the urban winery was mine and I had it long before I met Steve. He doesn't get to use it to make a chain of identical urban wineries in other towns. No, no, no."

"I am one hundred percent certain we'll be able to get this excused as a frivolous case in court." Alex clasps his hands together, his frustration seeping over the computer monitor. "Like I've been telling you, he doesn't have anything here for a lawsuit. It can be seen as harassment in the court of law."

"Ugh." I cradle my forehead in the palm of my hands. "This is nuts. The fact this has been able to get this far blows my mind."

"It happens more often than people think. People think they can sue for anything, and they try to. Some do it just to be mean...to harass someone and cause issues. I had this happen with a case over a hedge."

"Over a hedge? Like bushes?"

Alex's head bobs up and down. "We got the case dismissed as a frivolous lawsuit and the plaintiff had to pay my client, the defendant, a nice hefty fine plus all of their lawyer's fees."

"That's the kicker, isn't it? That as the defendant, I need

to retain a lawyer." Not that I could afford any of this right now, mind you. Steve had decided that not only could I not open another business like the one I used to have, but he also had held onto the money he owed me when I sold my share of the business. "Speaking of retaining—because retainers make me think of money, which makes me think of how I have none until this is over—how are we with getting him to release the funds he owes me?"

"His lawyer told me he isn't budging. We're going to have to wait for a judge to order him to release the funds." Alex tosses me a sad smile. "Wish I could do more right now, but we have to wait for our day in court."

"That doesn't make me feel better." I exhale the longest sigh of my life. "I need a nap."

"Uh-uh." Alex holds up a finger stopping me. "The last thing I need you to do right now, though, is to lie down and let this trainwreck of a situation run you over. You need to decide when—not if—the judge determines this is frivolous, what you want to do."

Confused, I fall back into the overstuffed cushions of my couch and shake my head back and forth. "What do you mean?"

"Defendants in cases like yours can turn around and sue the plaintiff for malicious prosecution. This includes suing for damages, and we can also tag on the harassment of the whole situation and, if you want to go further, we can talk about how it's affected your mental state."

"My mental state?" I look down at my feet, noticing for the first time in who knows how long that I need a pedicure. Does that count for my mental state? "I mean, if you're trying to say my mental health has been impacted..."

"Yes?" Alex says as he leans closer to his monitor.

I shrug my shoulders. "It really hasn't. I'm irritated, but I'm not losing sleep over it yet."

"Okay, well, I want to keep it that way." He smiles. "I'll be in touch if I need anything. Remember, if he reaches out, do not engage. Let the court handle this, okay?"

Closing my computer disconnects us, an end to a conversation I don't want to have anyway. If there is one word I hoped I'd never have to utter in my lifetime, it is the D word: divorce. I knew women when I lived in D.C. who approached getting married as something you can take on and take off, like a pair of jeans. Too tight? Get another pair.

Not me. At least I hadn't wanted that to be the tale to come out after my marriage, but unfortunately it is. The thing that has me so baffled here, though, is the fact Steve and I parted amicably after realizing we'd outgrown each other. I mean, it's not like we had a party when we split up—it was sad and we both hurt—but we'd remained business partners and chose to stay cordial with each other. It was a hard road, but I thought we'd gotten there...wherever *there* was.

A bark followed by some commotion on the other side of the living room steals my attention; my two schnauzers, Thor the traitor and Hercules, have tumbled to the floor, landing in a cuddle puddle of glory in a sunshine beam streaming through the living room window.

My heart always goes pitter patter when I see my dogs; they've been my sanity through all the chaos life has become. You can bet when I left D.C., these two were put in the car first. As long as I have them, I feel like I can handle anything.

My heart squeezes as I look around my little bungalow. It had taken me a little time to find a three-bedroom with a fenced-in yard, and this one was a steal due to the work that has to be done to it still. Work that one day I'll deal with, but right now the thought of renovating anything makes me break out in hives.

Outside, the world has been painted in an autumnal brilliance of golden strokes, touched with splashes of blazing orange, only to be further complemented by the most brilliant ruby reds as trees cover the ground with their leaves. Grinning, I wrap my arms around my middle knowing that the fall evening means only one thing: Mama is gonna light her fireplace tonight.

THREE
Zac

Since Hurricane Etta left the building yesterday, I've been trying to cleanse my mind of her. Something about that woman gets to me. Not in the kind of way that's bad, like poison ivy, but for some reason whenever I see her I feel a little hitch in my heart.

Etta McCoy is beautiful, and if someone asked if she was my type, I'd nod my head because she is absolutely my type. She's headstrong, fierce, independent...definitely not a pushover. However, I gotta be honest with myself—I think she scares me.

Now, I don't mean scared in the way where I tremble when I see her, out of fear, but more like scared because anytime I'm around her, I get this feeling. It's a humming sound that starts in my ears, blocking out all other noise. It swells to an eclipse, before it reverberates into my chest, pinging around inside that hollow cavity like a pinball, until it flows with the force of a garden hose turned up to the hilt, swirling and swooshing this chill through my body.

The stack of paperwork Sergeant Lane drops on my desk hits with a thud so intense, my teeth almost rattle. Almost.

But it does take me out of my daydream about she-who-shall-not-be-named.

Glancing up, I find him grinning my way as he pushes the stack closer to where I sit.

As I eye the pile suspiciously, I thumb a sheet of paper. "What's this?"

"This," he says as he pats the mound of documents and pulls a chair up on the other side of the desk, "is a project I really need your help with."

Leaning back in my chair, I fold my arms and settle in to listen. I'm the new man on the roster, so there's a lot of grunt work I'm asked to take the first run at. "What do you need?"

"Before you started working here, we found out that the state had allocated a nice chunk of funding for police departments. There is a project I've been wanting to start here for ages, but money has always been the issue."

Taking a folder off the top of the stack, he slides it over, the bold print on the front of it proclaiming "K9 MENTAL HEALTH UNIT PROJECT."

I pick up the folder and study it. "You want to get a canine unit in here?"

"No, not really." Lane leans over the desk. Taking me into his confidence, he whispers, "I want to have a few dogs available for mental health reasons only."

Well, now my interest is officially piqued. "I guess you saw on my resume I used to train dogs?"

"Guilty." He plants his elbows on my desk and clasps his hands. "You've got a ton of experience, and you can bet I want to use it."

"Fair enough. So, what's the project?"

"I want to be the first department in the state to have a Canine Comfort Therapy Team."

I nod my head in response. This could be a good idea in certain situations. "How do you see it working here?"

"Given the right circumstances, we'll have a facility where we house the dogs and have a training center for our officers. The idea being to eventually have officers from other departments around the state come and train with us, if we're successful with this initiative, that is—which I think we will be."

"You said given the right circumstances…I take it we don't have those?"

"Ahhh…" Growling, Lane crosses his arms in front of his chest as he sinks back in his chair. "Afraid not. Welcome to Sweetkiss Creek, the town that gets the scraps."

Chuckling, I wiggle my eyebrows. "But the name is so pretty."

"I know," he says. "But we're the pretty and forgotten cousin down the road, who really wants to make a difference. Do you know we have had more callouts in the last eighteen months for what the public deems as someone who is an extreme danger or considered a threat? Most of the time, with these kinds of calls, it's someone having mental health issues, and it's heartbreaking we can't do more."

I dip my chin in concession. "In my last job, we had a local army veteran who suffered from PTSD. He'd get worked up and no one knew how to talk him down, only his family could do it. One day, when he was having a fit over noise in his neighborhood, his daughter, who happened to be dog sitting, discovered the neighbor's dog calmed him."

My heart still swells at the thought. Speedy, the old guy's nickname, was now the proud owner of Bunny the cavoodle because of it.

"Then you get it. We need to do more for the vulnerable members of our community, not lump them into a one-size-fits all situation." Lane tips his head at the stack of paperwork. "All of that is literature for you to review, but I basically need someone to help me apply for this grant. Our annual charity ball fundraiser is in a few weeks, so we will have funds from that to get started. However, we need more if we want to build and maintain a facility. We've applied for this grant twice now, and no joy. I'm hoping this is a case of 'third time's a charm' with you across it."

Knowing his reasons why and seeing how I can help, my inner significance sits up much taller in its seat. "Let's see if I can work some magic, sir."

"Thanks, Wright." Sergeant Lane kicks his chair back and hops up, walking away only to turn around once more. "Oh, and did I see on your resume you took leadership classes and ran team activities with your department back in Beaufort?"

Seems that someone has been reading the manual of Zac. "Yes sir, you did. I was one of five who worked on a committee to coordinate our team retreats and bonding."

"Fantastic," he says as he claps his hands together. "You're our new team activity leader."

"What the...are you sure, sir? There must be someone else who's been here longer that would be better suited for the role." The look Lane shoots my way tells me another story. "Or maybe not. Maybe I should say thank you and simply ask who I'll be working with."

"I like you, Wright. You get it." Sergeant Lane laughs, sweeping his arm around the room. "If you need to form a committee, go ahead. You have your pick."

Officers are scattered, a few sit at their desks while some are out on calls. At least one, I think his name is Felix, is staring out the window. To be fair, it is a quiet day and the town of Sweetkiss isn't a metropolis, so we're a small team. A few of our crew are off work today, and of course, there's the ones I'm not thinking of who rotate out for night shifts.

I get the sense there's some sarcasm in Lane's laugh somewhere, though, but there's not enough time in the day for me to examine my suspicions. I'm the newbie, so I want to make... scratch that, I *need* to make a good impression.

Grabbing the stack of papers for the grant, I place them under my desk with my things to take home after work. A little light reading in bed tonight will do me some good anyway.

When I'm ready to finish up for the day, I lift my head and almost pass out when Tuck suddenly appears in front of me. "I'm back!"

"It's like you're a ghost, your vapor sneaking in here and suddenly you appear at my desk."

"Hey, you knew I was coming back." He glances at his watch, then back to me. "When I texted last night, you said five-thirty was a good time." He taps its face. "Five-thirty on the button. Are you free now?"

"I can be." Leaning back under the desk, I grab my things and hold them in the air, showing off my goods. "But I'll need to come back here after dinner to grab my things. I get to take homework with me."

Tuck peeks at the massive pile under the desk. "Confidential files? Mugshots? Maps to treasure?"

"Treasure? Where do you come up with these things?"

Tuck laughs, jerking his head toward the door. "Come on, let's go. I'm starving."

"There's a steakhouse down the street." Peeking out the front window, I see the sun is on its way down and, figuring the evening air is already crisp, I grab my jacket from the back of my chair and put it on. "You know the one, we've been there before."

"The Magnolia Grill, yeah." Tuck's eyes narrow, humor wrinkling at the edges. "Why are you telling me this?"

"Because you need to know where the finish line is," I say with a snicker as I take off faster than a toupee in a hurricane, not even pausing long enough to call out, "1, 2, 3, RACE!"

The clinking of glasses and low hum of conversation fills the air of The Magnolia Grill. We'd entered the restaurant, breathless, pushing each other out of the way in the door. As Tuck swipes at me and tries to pull me back, I manage to slip from his grasp and slam my hand on the hostess stand, thus scaring the living tar out of the sweet teenage girl who is working her shift.

"I win!" Arms in the air, I turn around triumphantly to find Tuck taking gulps of air and trying not to laugh. I spin around, back to the hostess, holding up two fingers and catching my own breath. "Two. Dinner. Please?"

The hostess is quick to lead us down the steps into the dining room and to our table near the window, giving us a menu each before taking our drink orders and quickly walking away.

"So, how's the new job so far?" Tuck asks, his breathing returning to normal as he peruses the menu.

"Busy." The hostess is back at our tableside, placing our drinks in front of us before disappearing again. I want to tell her I'm sorry we were so boisterous. I really need to be more adult since I live in this town now and I'm policing it. But it's hard to be an adult when my brother is in the vicinity. "My sergeant dropped a huge project into my lap today."

Tuck cocks his head to one side. "What is it?"

"He wants to start a Canine Comfort Therapy team."

"Like a K-9 unit?"

I shake my head. "It's a unit for mental health. In the past, counselors have advised a therapy dog would be good in call-outs where the case is sensitive or the person who we're responding to is in a vulnerable state."

Tuck raises one eyebrow. "That's a big project alright. What do you need to do?"

"Start by attacking the paperwork and getting to know the project, then I'll look into applying for a grant. Sergeant Lane wants enough money to set up an actual facility for training these kinds of units for the whole state."

"Oh, that would be so cool," Tuck says with a nod as he sips his cocktail. "Right up your alley. Did you tell them you used to be a dog trainer?"

"It's on my resume, so it's one of the reasons he asked me. It would be cool to be the person who has a hand in bringing an initiative like this to town, but I'm not going to lie. It feels daunting."

We're interrupted when our server appears, jotting down our order before she walks away. As she does, Tuck inclines his head in her direction.

"Dude...she totally looks like Laney. Right?"

Squinting my eyes, I try to catch another glimpse of her face as she walks through the dimly lit restaurant. "I can't tell."

"Keep watching. She's on the move again." Tuck inclines his head toward the other side of the restaurant near the hostess stand. "She's headed to greet someone at the door."

I'm so busy watching her thread her way to the front of the house that I don't even notice the person who she's about to greet. Not until my eyes lock with theirs.

Etta can't mask the irritation that flits across her face when she recognizes me. She bends closer to speak to the hostess, turning her back to me and to the rest of the restaurant, before she marches over to a couch in the lobby and sits down.

"Tuck, I'll be right back," I manage as I push my chair out and stand up.

I can feel his eyes boring a hole through my back as I work my way over to the lobby where Etta sits staring at me, boring a hole in my front. I'm going to be a tunnel by the time these two are done with me.

I take the four steps leading into the lobby quickly. So

quick, that I forget the last step is even there. The toe of my shoe catches, snagging on something coming out of the floor and I can't seem to pull my foot away.

Etta must have seen the look of shock appear on my face because I'm treated to her features turning from tranquil ambivalence into actual full-fledged fear as I'm launched into the air and am now weightless and falling forward.

I'll never understand why she thought she could help me, but in the confusion of it all, Etta stands—at the same time my face plants itself in her lap. I'm like a human flesh rocket or some kind of perverted heat-seeking missile.

By the time we land, I've somehow managed to end up on my back while embracing Etta and clutching onto her arms. I can smell the rage building inside of her as she pushes herself off of me only to cry out in pain and swat at the side of her head.

"Your watch is tangled in my hair," she hisses.

"Oh, sorry. I was trying to snag it in your sweater." Her face tells me she's not ready to laugh about this yet, and that's fine. I carefully pull a few stray strands of hair out of my watch band. "You should be free now."

As we finally climb to our feet, Etta shoots me a look that could kill. I'm pretty sure she's gearing up to rip me a new one when the hostess appears and hands Etta a brown bag with food to go.

Turning to face me, Etta puts one hand on her hip. "You are a hot mess."

I can't argue with her, but I'm allowed to think about how gorgeous she is when she's mad, right? "Etta, lucky for you, I'm a positive person."

"Why is that?" she huffs.

"Because," I manage with a wink, "I'm gonna focus on the fact you called me hot."

And if you're wondering if she stormed off after that one, I can say without a shadow of a doubt that yes, yes she did.

When I get back to the table, Tuck is chewing on his appetizer and trying not to laugh, but the fact his cheeks are bright red tells me he is loving the surprise dinner and a show part of his night.

"Wow, you certainly have made quite an impression here in Sweetkiss Creek…or is it Sweetkiss 'Crick'?"

Grabbing my silverware, I stab at my salad and shove a forkful in my mouth. I'm not ashamed to eat my feelings.

"It's a fluke, Tuck. An anomaly." I poke at my steak. "And it's only that woman. She's a handful. I'd compare her to a wet bee, but she's more like the whole hornet's nest."

"She seems sassy, but…" He whistles, keeping it low and sing-songy. "She's pretty."

A tiny arrow hits my heart when Tuck says this. I have noticed she's beautiful, but it shouldn't matter considering how insane she makes me. Yet when Tuck makes the comment, I feel a stab of something.

"Guess what I won?" Tuck interrupts my internal debate to pull a small envelope out of his pocket and slide it across the table toward me.

Opening the envelope, I pull out a flimsy baseball card and grin as I reminisce. As kids we both collected baseball cards—of course we had to do the same thing. It was what we did, what we still do. We have always had to one-up the other, so my childhood memories of the highs and lows of card collecting with Tuck in the house are still in technicolor for me. It was always war, in the way boys who are brothers can war. It was its own kind of ruthless.

"You know what that one is, right?" Tuck sits back in his chair, smiling like the Cheshire Cat in Alice in Wonderland.

Inspecting it a little closer, it hits me. "It's a '55 Bowman

Mickey Mantle." My jaw hits the table. "This was the card I wanted when we were little! Where did you get it from?"

Tuck's preenish grin tells me I've given him the reaction he so desperately needed. "I found out about a contest at a comic book store, of all places, last time I was in Virginia. There's a cool store right when you cross the border, and I always stop there because Laney likes the Buffy comic books... but I digress. Long story short, I entered and my name was pulled. Ta da!"

Only Tuck would win something this epic. Epic to us, but not to anyone else really...unless they were baseball card collectors, that is. "That card is worth, like fifty thousand dollars or something, isn't it?"

Tuck nods his head, jubilant. "It is."

Am I insane with jealousy? A little bit. And Tuck knows. "I can tell you like it, like you want it as bad as you used to want my car."

"I ended up with my own car, don't forget," I tap the table, punctuating my sentence. "I actually bought mine and didn't have to go to bank mom and dad."

"Semantics." Tuck laughs, grabbing the card from the table and sliding it back into its envelope. "You know, if we were to make a small wager, I may be willing to let this go."

"A small wager? That card is worth a lot of money." I shovel another load of salad in my mouth as I shake my head. "You're being ridiculous."

"It's not like I paid for it; I won it." The envelope is back on the table, Tuck's fingers dancing across it. "And toying with your emotions is fun. If you win this card, you complete your collection."

This man is a sadist, but he's right. "That collection was put away a long time ago." I slam back into my chair, crossing my arms in front of me. "I put my toys away when I left home, Tuck."

"This is not a toy, it's an investment. In you." He leans forward, putting his elbows on the table. "Come on. You know you want to do it. I bet you..."

"No." I then resort to the most mature thing I can think of. I place my hands over my ears. "No, no, no. Do not dare me. Do not double-dog dare me...don't dare me to do anything, at all anymore, ever."

"But it's such a gooooood daaaaare." He's almost pleading with me. This is why I love him. And hate him. And love to hate him...I guess it's why I hate to love him, too.

Is the competition so strong between us that this moment is a hard one for me to walk away from? Yes.

"Tuck, when we do this, things get crazy. It goes a few steps beyond sibling rivalry, and into a territory of chaos if we aren't careful. Which is why I'm saying no."

Tuck sighs, putting the card back into his pocket one final time. "You are so boring now that you're a cop."

"Boring gets to eat dessert."

Rolling his eyes, Tuck pushes his chair back and stands. "Fine, I'm going to the restroom. I need a moment to understand why you'd say no."

While Tuck walks away, I scan the room again, my eyes landing on the spot in the lobby where I lay tangled with Etta not that long ago. As I do, a clean, breezy floral scent assaults my senses, reminding me of her. Realizing that some of her perfume must have gotten on my clothing, my eyes dart around the room while I do a quick sniff check. Don't need the locals to think I'm smelling myself because I stink or smell funny.

Her scent is on my collar and my sleeve from where we had rolled to the floor together. It's heady, hitting me like a rush, but it also makes me smile as I remember the heat of her body against mine when I helped her up.

Seeing my brother making his way back, I take another

whiff of my collar, like taking a hit of something that's not quite legal, even closing my eyes to savor the moment. It's like my secret drug right now, and it makes my grin even wider.

This joyous aroma is everywhere...I am not mad about it at all.

FOUR

Etta

"Hold on," Riley says, wiping a tear from her eye. "His face landed in your lap? We need to tell someone at The Magnolia Grill they should charge extra for that."

Glaring at my supposed friend, I shove another container of food her way, sliding it across the kitchen counter like it's a hockey puck gliding across ice. Riley stops the out-of-control container before it slides off the edge and slams onto the floor below.

"I'm glad you find it funny, because I'm not amused." I wave my hands in the air around me. "I don't have time to argue with Zac or have his head accidentally end up in my lap or think about much else right now; I have enough going on. Have you seen the state of me and this place?"

"Well, you did say you wanted a fixer-upper." Riley shrugs her shoulders and points to the pile of sheets and plastic drop cloths in the corner. "And I see you've gotten some of your supplies finally. Which room is being painted first?"

"Living room and entryway this week." I'd decided to start painting because it would keep me busy. Could I hire a company to do it for me? Of course. In fact, several of the local kids had already offered to do it, and for a good price, but there's just something soothing in putting on a true crime podcast and being at home, painting your own house—at least, that's what I keep telling myself.

"You need to take before and after pictures." Following me, Riley takes a few plates of food into the living room, placing them on the coffee table. Caprese salad, hummus and tahini dips with grilled veggies, and two cobb salads. Perfect for our girls' night. Almost.

"We need one more thing." I slap my hands together and look at Riley. "Wine. Grab the glasses and I'll pick out a bottle."

Skipping down the hall, I go to grab a bottle of Malbec from my private stash, also known as my hall closet. I'd ordered a wine fridge a few weeks back, but it's not due here for another few days. Until then, my hall closet has to do.

Getting down on my hands and knees, I pull out a box and inspect a few bottles when the doorbell chimes. Riley answers the door as I scramble to my feet and walk back to the front of the house, thinking Amelia's joined us.

Instead, I find Riley holding a giant bouquet of flowers. Roses, lilies, tulips, lily of the valleys...you name it, I think the florist managed to stuff it in there. Taking the bouquet out of Riley's hands, I head back to the kitchen with her in tow. As soon as I place it on the counter, she gets busy looking for a card.

"Hey, did you know the front door is wide open?" Amelia calls out from the other room. "You guys in here?"

"In the kitchen." Riley's hand suddenly shoots in the air. "Found it!"

She hands me the tiny envelope as Amelia sweeps in, her eyes bouncing back and forth from Riley to me. "Obviously I closed the door, since you two hooligans can't. What is going on here?"

Riley grins. "Someone had flowers delivered."

"I can't remember the last time someone sent me flowers." I finally get the envelope opened and pull out the card inside. My heart drops into my stomach as soon as I see the name. I toss the card onto the counter, far away from me like it's a hot nuclear coal.

Amelia, her eyes on me, reaches out and takes the card, reading it out loud. "I wish it was different. Steve."

"Your ex?" Riley asks, one eyebrow slowly beginning to arch. I'll never figure out how she can do that and make it look so cool.

"The guy doesn't give up, does he?" Amelia tosses the card back to the counter, almost as fast as I had, but not quite. "Is he trying to play nice to get his way?"

Nodding, I take the flowers and move them to a small room off the back of the kitchen, an old closet I've designated to be my laundry room eventually. I don't want to look at the flowers, but I also don't want to toss them away, so out of view for now will do.

"He sent me fruit baskets when I was staying with my brother and Maisey, and he tried to send them to my grandmother, too. She's ornery, that one, and so she sent every package back." Casting my mind back to a few months prior, I also remember the basket of dog biscuits, new leashes, and other canine accessories that made their way to me as well. "Steve even sent stuff for Thor and Hercules, but we gave it to the local SPCA."

"Bribes. He's showering you with bribes." Amelia looks me up and down before grabbing my arm and pulling me into the living room. "Come on. It's time for you to sit down and chill out."

Riley pours us each a glass of wine, and we toast before

sitting down. My overstuffed chair calls me tonight, and I answer willingly, leaning back into its soft and plush goodness and closing my eyes.

"Where are the dogs?" Amelia asks after taking her first sip.

"They'll be home later." I hold my glass of wine up and grin. "I asked the dogwalker to keep them a little longer tonight so we don't have them begging for food while we eat."

"Thank goodness; they always make me feel so bad." Amelia giggles. She reaches over to take an empty plate, snapping her hand back as she looks at me. "Are we waiting for Dylan, or is she still on her honeymoon?"

Shaking my head, I lean forward and grab a plate myself and begin to fill it. "She and Reid are still out of town. It's just us tonight; we're down a member of the Fab Four."

"Are we taking the name away from the royals when we call ourselves the Fab Four?" Riley muses, and thoughtfully, too, I might add, while Amelia rolls her eyes.

"They are not the fab anything. *We* are the Fab Four." She looks pointedly at Riley. "Anyway, weren't you like a fair queen or something? Cause if that's the case, we have our own version of royalty sitting right here, folks."

"County fair princess. My parents wanted me to do it, and I think my mom would have loved it if I had gone the pageant route. It was something I grew out of quickly, though." Riley reaches forward, scooping some salad onto a plate and grabbing a fork. "I'm not the proper type. I don't want to have to hold my shoulders back and do the smiling thing."

I'm not sure if it's Amelia who starts laughing first or me, but we both grab for one another and fall into each other, giggling.

"Why is that so funny?" Riley manages to ask between bites.

"You like, literally, have the kindest and most level disposition of all of us." Amelia leans across the coffee table to where Riley has copped a squat on the floor and pats her head.

"I'm not that nice," Riley growls, only to start cracking up at herself. "Okay, I see what you mean. So if you ever need someone cuddled to death, I'm your girl."

"Me!" I thrust my hand in the air. "If I could have you cuddle my ex out of my life, I'd be so happy with that."

"I just don't understand why he thinks he can sue you for the business." Amelia leans forward to fill her glass, leveling her gaze with mine. "What is his reasoning?"

Sighing, I lean forward and put my elbows on my knees. "All was well after we divorced. It wasn't until I said I was moving that the business came up and he suddenly turned into someone I don't recognize."

"So things were fine between the two of you?" Riley queried.

"Yep. We were running the D.C. location and getting along really well. Then, I asked him if he wanted to buy me out. He agreed, and when he asked me what I was going to do next, I told him I was going to replicate the idea and open another urban winery here, in North Carolina. That was the instant he flipped. Next thing I knew, he lawyered up, saying the business was his idea and he wanted me to sign paperwork saying I would never open another winery like *his.*"

"Ooof." Riley shakes her head and locks eyes with Amelia.

"That takes some guts," Amelia says, shaking her head, too.

"It takes more than guts to do that, I'm telling ya." Sitting up a little taller, I smile at my two friends. "My lawyer says it's going to be seen as frivolous in the eyes of the court, and if anything, I'll be the one with the upper hand."

"But you still had to pay, what, a ten-thousand-dollar retainer fee in order to deal with being served?"

"Oh yeah." Hearing the dollar amount makes me sick to my stomach. "I had to borrow most of it from my family."

"That's right," Amelia murmurs. "He's also holding back the money he owes you, right?"

"Ding, ding, ding. You win a prize, caller!" My voice is light, but my heart is heavy. "Look, it hurts that he wants to take something I created from me, and no matter what the outcome is, it's always going to have a little sting because we were married at one time. I never could have seen this side of him coming. Hopefully, we can get past it quickly and then I can figure out how to open my wine shop down here."

"That's my girl!" Amelia holds her glass in the air. "Here's to that!"

"Ditto what Amelia said," Riley echoes with a grin. "I hate when people say this, but it's a very true statement: it is all going to work out. No matter what, I know you'll be taken care of."

"And," Amelia sings out as she stands up to come wrap her arms around me, "we're right here to catch you. No matter what."

Squeezing Amelia back, my insides surge with warmth. These women being in my corner means everything to me. One day, I'll be able to tell them how their strength gets me out of bed in the morning, but not now. One day soon.

"Okay." I clap my hands together. "I made dessert. And by made, I mean I stopped at the store and bought an apple pie I can throw in the oven."

Riley jumps up, guiding me back to my chair by the shoulders before taking my empty plate out of my hands. "You sit, I'll clear plates and go start dessert."

I'm too tired to argue, so I flop back down into the seat and face Amelia while Riley buzzes around us. "And how are you doing?"

Shrugging, she lifts her glass to her lips and takes a sip

before answering. "I'm good, except I need to put together a team training event for a local group, and I need to do it soon."

"Congrats on booking a group at the campground," Riley calls out as she disappears into the kitchen.

Amelia moved to Sweetkiss Creek about a year ago, and since then, she and her movie star husband, Spencer Stoll, have been making their mark. They've been building their dream home on the lake, managed to open an art gallery, and bought the local campground. Sweetkiss Creek is getting a makeover, whether it wants one or not.

"Thanks, it's the first big booking since Dylan and Reid's wedding." I watch as her shoulders visibly relax and she allows herself to fall back into the couch cushions. "Oh man, this sofa is comfy."

"I know, I do all of my best thinking there."

"So team building, huh?" Riley asks as she struts back in the room. "Is it like the escape room that's in town?"

Amelia catches me shuddering at the memory of the escape room. Look, it's a fun place to go. I happened to end up there on a double date with the worst person ever: Zac. If Zac only knew how cute he is, borderline hot even—until he opens his big mouth. Thanks to him, it was an impossible evening with the two of us arguing our way through the escape room for sixty minutes of my life that I will never get back.

But, the other couple on the date with us, Dylan and Reid? Worked for them; they're married now.

I shake the memory off and turn my attention back to the room and to Amelia, who's speaking.

"It's kind of like that, I guess? I don't know, I have never had to organize one of these before. I was actually going to ask the two of you if you had any ideas about team building events."

Riley shakes her head. "I've never been to one or seen one, so I got nothing."

"We did them at the winery," I offer. "We had so many different personalities working there, so we tried to do team building every six months to keep our crew tight. It works."

Amelia's eyes light up. "Really? What kind of exercises did you do with them? Because that's exactly what I need. Someone who can help me organize events for these folks to run through and possibly help me by running the whole program."

"Have you asked Dylan?" I may be throwing my absent friend under the bus, but she does live on the campgrounds.

Amelia nods slowly. "She's not available. She and Reid won't be back from their epic trip in time."

"Must be nice to take off for a month on your honeymoon," Riley says as she sits back down on the couch. "So if she's not around, did she maybe suggest anyone for you to try asking?"

Smiling a tight, almost creepy smile, Amelia turns in her seat to face me. "She did."

"What are you doing," I say, pointing to her mouth, "with your face?"

"I'm trying to warm you up to the notion that maybe you could be the one I bring in to help with this event?"

As soon as the words are out, she goes back to the creepy grin again. It actually reminds me of porcelain dolls—and I'm not a fan. I cut my eyes away, but look back only to find her eyes wider and her grin showing more teeth.

I throw my hands in the air. "Stop doing that and I'll do whatever you need."

"Yay!" Amelia's up again, hugging me one more time. "Thank you, thank you. You're hired and you start tomorrow."

"Tomorrow?" This woman does not play.

Amelia's head bobs up and down. "We're meeting to go over the activities, they want to walk the site and go over catering...all that fun stuff. It's not too soon, is it?"

"No. It all sounds good to me." I stand up and grab some of the dishes off the table, clearing them to take to the kitchen. "As long as this crew doesn't have anyone like Zac Wright in it, we'll be just fine."

FIVE
Etta

Pulling up the next morning for my first day of work with Amelia, I have two dogs barking their heads off in my car. Not the first impression I want to make, but sadly, it's the only one I've got.

I steer my Volkswagen Beetle into a spot at the very back of the visitor parking lot and check my watch. I'm thirty minutes earlier than I need to be, and that's on purpose. I grab my phone and text Amelia so she knows I'm here, then let the dogs out to run in the woods by the campground.

As a single furbaby owner, making sure these two are exercised and happy is my human job, so when my dog walker called out sick today, did I get a little over-the-top worried? Indeed, but when I turn around and look in the back seat at these two precious muppets, my heart skips. I know they'll be less crazy at home tonight because they had a chance to get their energy out.

My phone beeps with Amelia texting me back that it's all good, I can drop them in the backyard behind Dylan's cabin. Dylan lives on site and acts as the campground manager for Amelia and Spencer. Thank goodness, as a dog owner herself, she's already a fan of Thor and Hercules and they've been here before, so I'm sure she won't have a problem with it.

I grab my backpack and we take off. I spend a good twenty minutes tramping through the woods to work their extra energy out of their systems before turning around and heading back. I make a detour on my way out of the trees and head to Dylan's cabin. Getting them in is the easy part, sneaking away without them freaking out could be an issue.

The two brothers race around the yard, then head to a spot on the back porch where Dylan's made a makeshift bed out of an old comforter for her terrier, Max, judging by the size. My two ding-dongs slam into one another in their efforts to settle down, finally coming to a silent agreement where they curl up together, nose to tail, and pass out in a pillowy cloud of comfort.

Satisfied my human job is done, I sneak out the fence gate, making sure to close the latch behind me.

Glancing across the parking lot, I see Amelia crank her arm in the air and wave in my direction. Beside her stands another person, a man, who I'm guessing is the client, so I start jogging to get to them quicker. I get a feeling of familiarity when I see him, but my thoughts are interrupted by Amelia.

"I guess the dogs are secure?" she asks as I trot up beside her.

"Well, the latch closed." Crossing my fingers, I grin her way. "Here's hoping."

"Well, then we can get started." Amelia turns to the gentleman beside her. "Craig, this is Etta. She'll be the coordinator for your team building events. She's a former business owner herself who spent time organizing team building activities for her own employees."

Craig thrusts his hand out, shaking mine heartily. "It's nice to meet you officially, Etta. I'm here for the start of this meeting only because the person I've put in charge of this is at another appointment, but he'll be here soon."

"Gotcha." I swing my backpack off my shoulder and open it, pulling out a notebook and pen. I discard the bag beside Amelia's car, pull my hair back into a ponytail, and start making notes. "Can you tell me approximately how many will be in your group?"

Amelia points to a picnic table nearby and we follow her in that direction. Craig pulls out his phone.

"I have the final number confirmed in an email." He sits, scrolling his phone for a moment before tapping its screen and stopping on something of interest. Squinting his eyes, he scans his phone before his eyes light up. "There it is. We'll have twelve members of our team taking part."

I scribble this down. "I like twelve, it's a good number." When I look up, two pairs of eyes are staring at me like I'm speaking Greek. "What I mean is, this number of people allows you to go deeper in your team bonding. When you get over fifteen or sixteen people, I've found it harder to get them into a groove, you know?"

Beside me, Amelia nods. "I get it."

"That's a reasonable argument to me," Craig says with a grin as the cellphone in his hand beeps. He glances at the screen before putting it down. "Oh good, my coordinator should be pulling in any second."

"Before he gets here, let's head up to my office and sign the contract. Etta can stay here and wait for your guy," Amelia states as she hops up from the picnic table. She points to the building beside us. "The first floor of this building is our kitchen for the campground, but my office is upstairs."

Craig looks my way and after I nod, letting him know I'm fine with staying, he unravels himself from the picnic table and follows Amelia. "Let's do it."

My eyes trail behind them as they head inside. Once they

disappear from sight, I go back to my notebook and start making notes. I wasn't joking; knowing the number of people who are coming is beneficial because now I can start making a list of ideas for exercises and icebreakers we can take them through.

I have no idea how long I'm left alone. I can tell you it's long enough that I'm able to fill a page of my notebook on one side and half of the other before I'm brought out of my trance from the sound of tires crunching on gravel as someone makes their way up the driveway.

Looking up, I'm surprised to see a Sweetkiss Creek squad car slowly making its way up the lane and into the parking lot. My gut reaction at first is that something's wrong, and my second thought—now that I know he likes to escape—is that Thor got out again, only this time I know for certain where he is.

I glance up at the window to Amelia's office and there's no movement, so either she's not worried or she's not expecting them. Seeing as I am her temporary help, I jump up and walk around to the parking lot to see who it is.

As I do, a weird feeling hits my stomach. Looking up at Amelia's office window again, I realize I never asked Craig where he works. Nor did I ask who the team retreat is for. There's a sizzling feeling in the pit of my stomach as I think about all of the cruel jokes fate could play on me.

One would be having Zac Wright show up here today as the team coordinator for the police department. Even I can laugh at this thought because there is no way that it would happen.

None.

None at all, no way, not ever.

With these thoughts fresh in my mind, you can bet that when I walk around the front of the building, I am thinking every horrible thing one can imagine when I see Zac Wright climbing out of his cruiser, green eyes flashing my way and waving a hand in the air.

"You tricked me."

"No," Amelia manages through the clenched teeth of a fake smile she has plastered on her face. "You didn't ask. I didn't need to tell you, and to be fair, I didn't know Zac would be the coordinator. I've only dealt with Sergeant Lane."

While Amelia is able to serve up a faux grin for her visitors, which I chalk up to her experience with a husband who is also an actor, I cannot. Etta and "poker face" are three words not said in the same sentence often. Unless I'm dancing to Lady Gaga's song, then it's probably "Turn off Poker Face because Etta's dancing and we need her to stop."

But I digress. Let me fill you in.

As soon as Zac waved at me, I did what any reasonable and very adult woman would do: I walked straight to the campground kitchen building, opened the door, and marched upstairs to Amelia's office.

I'll be honest, I had no clue what I'd do once I got to the office, I just knew it was going to involve a serious talking to... because that's all I could do. As I was about to open her office door, Sergeant Lane flung it open from his side, stepping back in surprise. I'm pretty sure I mumbled something like "your other half just pulled up" as he went down to the parking lot to meet Zac.

Leaving me alone, in a room, with Amelia. The woman who will be known from this day forward and deemed as "traitor." I'm dramatic, what can I say? I'm also realizing I'm in a bad mood pretty much all the time, but hey, I'm getting used to this state of mind.

I opened my mouth to speak, but instead of being a friend

who was going to listen, Amelia grabbed her clipboard and brushed past me, telling me to follow her.

Which leads us to now, this moment where we're walking side by side across the grass to where Zac is standing with Sergeant Lane as I fight the urge to wrestle her to the ground.

The fact Amelia is brushing this off tells me I need to fall in line, and fast. I can handle being not happy with this situation for a little longer, and tell her after they leave that it's not going to be a good idea for me to be the point person, representing her, with Zac. At the end of the day, it's Amelia's business and I don't want to be the jerk that screws it up for her—by opening my mouth and telling Zac what I really think of him or, you know, helping him take a long walk off a short dock or something of the like.

"Now that we're all here, we should walk the site and discuss locations you want to use. You haven't said if this is going to be overnight, Craig?" Amelia flashes her supermodel-perfect grin their way. She's the kind of person that it wouldn't surprise me to find out she likes to tame wild unicorns and save koala bears in her free time. "We have a few cabins that are two-bedroom setups but can sleep up to six adults, as well as a cabin with bunk style sleeping arrangements for twenty-four people."

"It's going to be overnight." Zac Wright enters the conversation, ladies and gentlemen! "Ideally, we'll arrive in the late morning and get settled, have lunch, then start on team activities."

"Is it okay if we leave by lunchtime the next day?" Craig, AKA Sergeant Lane, asks as he crosses his arms in front of him. "I can arrange shifts around that time frame on my end for work. Plus," he says, leaning closer to Amelia, "if this goes over well, we'll be back with the other officers from the department that can't make it to this retreat."

"Sounds like a plan." She points across the grounds

toward the lake. "Let's walk that way, over to the tree line, and I can show you the cabins." She turns to Zac, pointing a thumb at me. "You should talk to Etta and rattle off any ideas you have for your event; she'll write it all down. Won't you?"

My eyes lock with Amelia's, and in that moment, the very moment I see laughter behind her peepers, I realize she knows what she's doing. When this is over, I'm totally going to kill her. She knows I find this man to be too much. He is flashy, a know it all, and a true pain in my derriere.

Yet, as I watch him walk away, straggling a little behind Amelia and his boss, my underlying irritation is drowning in the fact that he's actually not that bad to look at. So at least there's that, but he can't pull the wool over my eyes. I still hate him.

"Etta, you coming?" Amelia's voice snaps me out of my day-mare, my new made-up word for having a nightmare that you live through in the daytime. Clutching my clipboard, I jog twenty feet or so to catch them.

This is going to be the longest meeting of my life.

Ever.

SIX
Zac

You know the feeling you get when someone can't stand you? It's a feeling I've not felt since Christa Wallace in the fifth grade. I sat beside her in most of our classes because we sat alphabetically. Therefore, since Wright and Wallace were usually the only two "w" last names in the room, we would end up being near one another.

All that year, she would get mad at me for simply breathing. It felt like I never did anything right for her, and trust me, the fact that I felt these feelings as a kid and I still hold onto them now as a grown man should tell you something.

Now, standing here watching the back of Etta's head—because she refuses to look at me—I'm taken back to that time. I came home super sad one day that Christa was being so mean to me, and while my dad told me to just ignore it, it was my mom who really threw me for a loop. She looked me in the eye and said, "Zac, I think it's Christa's way of telling you she likes you. I'm not saying it's the right way, but sometimes people do weird things that are out of character to who they really are when love is involved."

So now, as Etta turns my way to make sure I'm following

her as we trod around the campground, I'm reminded of Christa Wallace and her immature way of showing me she liked me. I heeded my mother's advice and Christa became my girlfriend eventually. It may have lasted only two weeks, but hey...Mom was right.

I wonder what Mom would say about Etta? She'd probably compare Etta to a bucking horse, advising me to cinch up the saddle, make sure it's Western and not English, and make sure I hold on tight.

"This area is for any campfires you want to burn," Amelia says, stopping in front of a giant fire pit. "I figure if you're staying overnight and the weather stays September-perfect, you're going to want to light one."

"Great idea," I pipe in. Since I'm the one who's coordinating, I need to open my mouth and pay attention and stop staring at little Miss Sunshine beside me. "I think we should do s'mores. They pair nicely with a fire pit, don't they?"

"Ohh, great idea." Amelia grins my way, flicking a hand in the air while Sergeant Lane bobs his head up and down beside her. "Etta, add that to our grocery list?"

"You bet." Etta's voice drips with overt Southern sweetness. I can feel her eyes rolling into the back of her head. When I turn to face her, she's scribbling away in her notebook. She's either taking some super detailed notes, or she's doodling in order to keep her focus on her paper so she doesn't have to engage with me.

I take a step to get closer to her. "Can we request cinnamon-sugar graham crackers?"

"What?" Etta's head snaps in my direction, bringing with it a heady floral scent. Must be her shampoo.

"Cinnamon and sugar graham crackers. They sell them at Grocer Jim's in town." Etta doesn't write this down, so I point to her notebook. "Go ahead, make a note, please."

Only Etta doesn't move. Dragging eyes flashing with mild

rage away from mine, she looks pointedly at Amelia. I know women have this second nature way of communicating, but it seems Amelia didn't get the memo.

Amelia's face twists in confusion as Etta bugs her eyes out, primate-like. She flicks her gaze my way, then looks back at Amelia. Back to me, then back to Amelia. Finally Amelia and I lock eyes and she throws her hands in the air.

"Oh my g…of course, we can get you some cinnamon and sugar graham crackers. Etta's responsible for the grocery list, so she's got it handled." Amelia crosses her arms and stares pointedly at Etta. "Right, Etta?"

Pursing her lips together, Etta's cheeks flush pink. Did I push it too far? Honestly it's not what I want to do, but she's making me crazy. Just like Christa used to do.

She scribbles some notes before clutching the notebook close to her chest, averting her gaze from mine. "Done."

"Good." Amelia turns back to Lane, whose phone chimes, signaling a text. Lane whips his phone out of his pocket and checks the screen before looking at Amelia.

"Sorry to do this, but do you have a landline I can use?" He holds up his phone. "My signal is spotty down here, and I need to call in and let the team know we're a go for the retreat next week."

"Of course, I'll show you where it is," Amelia says, looking back at Etta. "Why don't you and Zac go over details of what he thinks he'll need and get that taken care of? And play nice."

Amelia, the smart woman she is, turns around before Etta can react and takes off with Lane in tow behind her.

Spotting a picnic table by the lakeside, I tip my head in its direction. "Mind if we sit?"

Without so much as looking in my direction, Etta marches over to the picnic table and takes a seat. Shaking my head, I follow and park myself in a position across from her.

"So," Etta hisses as she plants her hand firmly on her notebook and finally drags her eyes to mine. "Details?"

"You are a woman of many words, Etta McCoy, aren't you?"

Silence.

"Okaaaay." Half of me wants to laugh, the other half is in disbelief that an adult woman can be this stubborn. And cranky. Man, she's cranky. "You want details. I'll start with food. Let's see...we'll arrive midday and want a light lunch, please. Maybe a brown bag so we can get started right away. Also, we'll need a late afternoon snack, dinner, and breakfast the next day."

Etta nods, too busy to look my way (Ha. In my dreams.) as she takes notes. "Okay. And the s'mores, obviously."

"Obviously."

"Be good to get a list of any food allergies anyone may have, too." Etta finishes her last note, puts her pen down, and looks at me. "Gluten, dairy, and all that jazz."

"Who would be allergic to Chicago?"

The quirk of her lips is the tiniest of quirks if ever there was a tiny quirk in the world, but it's a quirk nonetheless.

"I'd hope no one, because Chicago is a great musical. I'm tempted to say the best, but..."

"But...what?" She's engaging, folks, and I'm not going to try to stop her and remind her she hates me.

Etta shrugs, and as she does, the loose top she's wearing slides down her arm, revealing her tanned shoulder. At this moment, I cannot help my eyes as they slide their way down her neck and across her shoulder, my heart happy when she doesn't try to pull the fabric back up.

"I'm more of a fan of Les Misérables myself." Still no smile, but we have comms people. "I know it's silly..."

"I think Cats is the one that most true Broadway enthusiasts see as silly, isn't it?"

"Huh." Etta cocks her head to one side. "Now that you mention it, yes."

"Well, would you look at that?" I acknowledge.

Etta's brow furrows as she glances over her shoulder. "Look at what?"

"We're talking like people do when they get along."

Glowering, Etta shakes her head. "Don't ruin it."

"Don't tell me don't ruin it. That ruins it." I shake my head back, wagging a finger in her direction. "It's like if I told you to calm down when you really don't want to calm down, or maybe you are calm and the fact I tell you to calm down is condescending."

"I feel like you're an overthinker," she hisses.

"An overthinker who knows magic," I say, wiggling my eyebrows.

Etta shakes her head. "I wouldn't advertise that."

"If we have a talent show for the retreat, maybe you'd be my stunning assistant?"

She stares at me, serving up a perfect blank expression. "We're not doing a talent show."

"It's not your retreat," I challenge.

"But it's at my campground."

"Not your campground." We really need some adult supervision here.

"Fiiiine." Etta huffs out a giant breath as she turns her eyes toward the heavens. "If you want a talent show, then we'll set something up, but no," she says, holding up one finger. "I will not be your assistant."

"Fine. I'm not a magician anyway."

Etta picks her pen up again, printing the words "talent show" onto a blank page in front of her before she slowly drags her eyes to meet mine, with a tiny smile playing on the ends of her lips.

And I'm not prepared.

This. Woman. She's like fried food—you know you shouldn't eat it, but whatever it is, it's going to taste good so you crave it. I understand this feeling because I've craved many things in my lifetime. Time alone, someone to hold, baseball cards...I feel things.

But right now, I'm feeling something new, something that at once takes my breath away as much as it blows life back inside of me. In this sheer millisecond of time, when Etta puts her pen down, cocks her head to one side, and stares at me, I feel like I'm seeing a wonder of the world for the first time—not that I've seen any of the wonders of the world or that I could name any right now, but I can Google it later.

When I think about the first night I met her, when my old roommate Reid tried to set us up on a double date, I thought she was gorgeous. Her eyes are a teal-blue I'd never seen before, and at that time, her hair was lighter. She was more of a strawberry blonde, not the dark auburn she's changed to. The fact doesn't escape me that I'm remembering every detail of meeting her for the first time like it was yesterday, and the thought makes me smile a grin so wide, I can feel it stretching from ear to ear.

I'm still lost in thought when Etta taps my hand.

"Hey," she hisses, her voice authoritative. Or it could be frustration, not sure. "Are you even listening to me?"

"What?" Hoisting one shoulder, I feign innocence, struggling with the fact that I've probably been staring at her with my mouth wide open for the last sixty seconds or so.

Etta's face contracts into tight lines, her teal-blue eyes swirling with thunderstorms now. I think we've got a tornado unleashing this time.

"I said, if you want to do a talent show and do it right, I can arrange for a stage to be put in the dining area, but I need to know today because I have to order it from the events company." She eyes me, folding her arms stubbornly in front of herself.

"We don't need a stage because we're not having a talent show." You know, I don't think she's a tornado this time because it's hurricanes, I think, that are affected by the turning of air from hot to cold and back, causing turbulence in the atmosphere. Another tidbit I'll need to research later. "I was joking."

The moment she levies a glare my way is the moment I want to rewind the day and start over. To call said look poison-tipped is doing it a disservice because she has managed to get all of her thoughts and feelings into one stare. Deciding I'd rather have her for me than against me, I open my mouth to apologize, but I'm interrupted when Amelia and Lane rejoin us.

"We're done here for now, Wright," Lane decrees as he slaps me on my back. "I need to get back. I have a meeting in ten minutes and these two ladies don't need us taking up any more of their time."

"No trouble, Craig. It's been nice talking with you," Amelia all but purrs. She doesn't wait for me to extend my hand before grabbing it and pumping it a few times. My back is to the picnic table, and when I turn around to say goodbye to Etta, I find her already up and making her way at a fast clip across the grass headed to the main building.

"Nice chat," I say to no one as I grab my keys out of my pocket and trudge to my car.

We only have to work together for a few days, that's all. I may be a glutton for punishment, but maybe...just maybe...I can figure out a way during our time together to get Etta to notice me.

Maybe.

SEVEN
Etta

I don't need persuasion to get my dogs in the car, like some people do. I just need to say two words. Two very important words that get these guys going every time. Dog. Park.

As soon as these words fall off my lips, I get instant insane schnauzer mode. We're talking spinning, barking, jumping, and even some running in circles. Two sets of eyes will follow me as I swipe leashes from their hooks, grab my bag, and head out the door. By the time I've locked the door and turned around, Thor and Hercules are always at the car door stomping their tiny feet with excitement.

The dog park is already bustling with midday activity when I pull into the lot. I snag the first empty spot, putting my car in park and looking around to see if I recognize anyone else's cars...or their dogs for that matter. I'm rewarded when I see Riley sitting on "our" bench and waving. Waving back, I open the door and let my two little guys out of the back seat, clipping leashes to collars before heading her way.

Once we're in the fenced area, I quickly unclip their leashes and let my little furry men fly, walking toward Riley as they pivot and take off running in the opposite direction. Ahhh, kids.

"Fancy seeing you here," she says with a giggle as I scoot in on the seat next to her. "I hear you and Amelia had a fun meeting yesterday."

"Ugh." I can feel my brows compressing over my eyes. "Is this a case of bad news traveling fast?"

"I don't think so." Riley angles herself on the park bench so she's facing me, feigning seriousness. "But I can't be sure really, since Amelia couldn't stop laughing when she told me that Zac showed up and now you have to work with him."

"I'm glad you two can laugh about it." Huffing, I throw myself against the back of the bench. "I just want to get through it."

Riley reaches into the giant tote bag sitting on the bench beside her and pulls out a bottle of water, handing it to me before pulling one out for herself. "So, Amelia saying you were being nice by the end of the meeting is a bit of a stretch?"

I take a sip of my water before answering. "Look, Amelia's asked me to help and I said yes. She's paying me for a professional job, so I'm going to be a professional for her."

Riley's eyebrows, in stark contrast to mine, flick upward. "I'm not going to act like I envy you, because no one wants to work with someone they can't stand, but at least as far as men go," she says as she nudges me with her elbow, "Zac is hot."

Closing my eyes, I take a giant sip of air and hold it before slowly expelling it, counting to five as I do.

Why? Because Riley isn't wrong about Zac—and that's another problem.

I'm not so focused on hating him that I hadn't noticed the firm sculpt of his biceps or how they flex when he holds Thor. Did I feel a pang inside when he smiled at me yesterday while showing off his Broadway musical knowledge, making me gulp a quiet but steadying breath?

Perhaps.

However, I'm not going to admit out loud I think Zac Wright is a good-looking man. In fact, I've had that thought since the day we first met and so far I've managed to keep my lips shut.

"If he only knew how cute he is"—I serve Riley my best sidelong glance—"until he opens his mouth. Then it's ruined."

"Oh, stop it." Riley's laughter echoes across the park. She takes a long, slow sip of water before shrugging off her lightweight jacket. "It's nice to feel the sun on my skin today. What's on your agenda this glorious Friday?"

Glorious. Only Riley could pull that word out and make it sound like it's trending. "Amelia's texting me a shopping list for next week so I can stock up on supplies. Once I have those errands out of the way, ummm...I'm home tonight and planning on painting the house at least one day this weekend."

"Ohhh, hold on." Riley thrusts her hand back inside her tote bag, pulling out her phone this time, which she scrolls through quickly. "Let me check my calendar. Yes! I'm free this weekend, so I should be able to give you a hand if you need one."

"I would love that, but please know if you change your mind it's totally cool." I play-jab her in the ribs with my elbow. "I've got my true crime podcasts to keep me company."

She scowls. "I worry about you listening to those."

"I'm not listening for an education or inspiration, so don't worry." My eyes are drawn to a stray fingernail that needs to be filed. I make a mental note to treat myself to a manicure once the painting is done. "My therapist used to tell me anxious people, like myself, listen to those podcasts or watch TV shows about crime because they need to understand they have some control of life—control to turn off the TV, to change the radio station."

"Control of their life to make a change." Riley eyes me as she nods with a restrictive enthusiasm. "While you make sense, it's still weird."

I lift a blasé shoulder and wink. "Maybe I was a private detective in another life."

"Or the village idiot," Riley muses as I smack her arm. "Ow!"

"That's what you get." Riley's also about to get an earful of me teasing her, but my phone saves the day and beeps on the bench beside me. A quick glance informs me it's Amelia, so I grab it to flick through the list.

"Why isn't Amelia going shopping for supplies?" Riley asks as she peers at the screen over my shoulder.

"Because she's flying out in a few hours to meet Spencer in New York." I put the phone down to look at Riley. "His new film premieres this weekend, so she agreed to walk the red carpet with him."

"Ooof. They've been fighting so much. Has she told you what's going on?"

I nod, a pit in my stomach forming. Amelia is a new friend for us, but she's fast become a good one since she moved to the area. "She said they were going to talk about a trial separation, but not until after he finishes with the press for this film, but that's all she wanted to say. For now."

"We'll have to have a girls' night when she's back," Riley says as she scans the dog park. "I swear, I thought I saw Max over that way a second ago..."

I indicate across the grassy space, where my two schnauzers are chasing the terrier in question around some trees. "Over there, with my two. Is he acting out because he misses Dylan?"

Riley giggles. "Man, having a dog is like having a kid. You guys never let on all the responsibility that happens here."

"Being a dog owner is serious business." I look at my watch. "Speaking of business, do you work today?"

Riley works part time for her family at their cafe in town. It's a great spot, and I know she's liked working there, but for Riley it's a dead end street. She sighs, her shoulders slouching as she nods her head.

"Yeah, I need to go actually. I told my parents I'd be there by one." Jumping to her feet, she puts her fingers in her mouth and whistles, one of those good, strong and loud whistles to get Max's attention. It works, with Thor and Hercules trailing behind him.

I grab my things and walk toward the gate that frees us into the parking lot. Once we're all on the other side, Riley wraps me a giant hug.

"I'll come by tomorrow, late morning, to give you a hand, okay?"

I pull away laughing and shaking my head. Riley is the kind of person who is so amazing and generous with her time, I wouldn't be surprised if she'd already promised her help to someone else, which is why I keep giving her an out.

"I'm willing to bet you fifty bucks you've forgotten you promised your mom's cousin's next door neighbor that you'd come by to help them set up their internet." When I'm met with a stone-faced demeanor, I lean in and give her another squeeze. "Come on, it's one of the things we all love about you."

"Yeah, yeah," she says with a grin. "I'll show you. I'll even bring the coffee."

"It's a deal." I say, flicking my hand in goodbye.

If she only knew my fingers were crossed behind my back.

After tossing a shopping bag into the trunk of my car, I pull my phone out and tick off another item on Amelia's to-do list. So far, I'd stocked up on pens and paper, gotten extra linen for the bunk house, managed to pick up supplies I need for the activities I'm planning from the local dollar store—where everything is really one dollar and twenty-five cents—and now I need to organize our firewood.

Luckily, we have Love Valley Firewood in town, your one-stop shop for all the wood and kindling you need. I zip into their parking lot and dash inside to give Mr. Burrall, the owner, our order, arrange the drop off, and then I'm back out again all in less than five minutes. This is when small-town living can be amazing. When you need to get a lot done in a small amount of time, you can.

I hop back in my car and glance at the clock on the dashboard and have a mild panic attack. I have fifteen minutes to get to the paint store before they close for the weekend and it's ten minutes away, fifteen if there's a tractor on a back road.

Drumming the steering wheel with my fingertips, I don't think about it for too long. I throw my car in reverse and take off. If I can get there close enough to the time they're closing, I may be able to beg Mr. King, the owner, to sell me the supplies I need.

I'm too busy berating myself over my lack of time management to notice the car that's gaining speed on mine. By the time I glance up in my rearview mirror, the police officer behind the wheel of said car has turned the lights on. I'm no speed demon by any means, but a sneak peek at my odometer tells me I'm going five miles over the speed limit. I fight the urge to scream.

Seeing as we're on a back country road and there's no one else around, I shake my head and flick the switch to indicate right, pulling my car over to the side of the road as soon as I deem it to be safe. At the rate I'm going, I'll never get to the store on time and painting will be put off again.

While I wait for the officer to come to my side of the car, I reach over and pull out my wallet with my driver's license and grab the car registration. Movement from behind causes me to flick my eyes toward the rearview mirror—and I watch in what feels like slow motion as Zac Wright sashays his way to my driver's side window.

I decide to wait for him to tap on the window to be let in, or invited in by me, if you will.

You know, like a vampire. I sit still, staring straight ahead with my right hand on the steering wheel and my left holding the documents I know he'll ask for.

The knock on the window I've been expecting comes. Tap, tap. I take a breath, and close my eyes as I do, wanting to give Zac the full effect of my irritation. Tap, tap, tap. Summoning all of the Zen power from the goddesses who have walked this earth before me, I turn my head slowly as I hit the button on the center console to roll my window down.

I shove my license and registration through the window. "I think we both know you just want the pure joy of writing me a ticket right now, so here you go." I wave my license and car registration in the air. "The address on my license hasn't been changed to my new house, though."

"It's not like I knew it was you or like I want to do this, especially not today." Zac takes off his sunglasses and steps closer to my window, taking the paperwork out of my hands. "Do you even know why I pulled you over?"

Controlling the rolling of my eyes, I nod my head. "I was going over the speed limit, and I'm sorry." I point to the clock on my dashboard. "But, I really needed to get to King's Paints before they close today."

"Everything is still registered in D.C." Zac inspects my license and registration, holding them close. "You need to change the address on both your license and car reg as soon as possible. We both know you've been here for more than sixty days, and that's the time limit."

Is this man for real? "Seriously, Zac. Can you just give me my ticket for speeding?"

Zac shakes his head. "You know, if I wanted to be a jerk, I could give you a ticket for both of these official documents not being up to date."

I swear, I can actually hear Mr. King's footsteps in my mind as he walks across the hardwood floors of his shop to close the door for the night.

"What's stopping you?" I say, a bit too grumpy for Zac's taste judging by his reaction.

He takes a breath and turns his face toward the sky. As he does, a tiny pit (see definition of tiny) forms in my stomach. One thing I do know, and I learned it from my mother, is that you don't catch bees with vinegar. Or maybe it's flies? Not like it matters. Maybe I'm the jerk and I'm pushing this comedy bit between us too far.

Toning down my immaturity a notch, I reach out and place my hand on his forearm.

"Sorry. I'm a bundle of nerves right now. I promise as soon as I go home, I'll figure out what time on Monday morning I can get into the DMV so I can sort all of this out."

"Really?" Zac slopes his head to the left, narrowing his eyes like he doesn't believe me.

"Hand on heart," I say as I do just that. "Look, I'll take whatever fine it is I need to pay. I just need to get to King's before they close."

Zac's eyes search mine when this tiny little sparkler goes off inside of me. There's a direct line of energy running from this man straight up my hand that's touching his arm, and directly into my core. I drag my eyes away from Zac's to look at my hand on his arm before snapping it back to the safety of my lap.

Glancing at his arm, he clears his throat and takes a step back. "As long as you do that, we should be fine. But, I still need to call this in. Give me a few minutes and we'll get you on your way."

I watch out the side mirror as Zac starts back to his car. He stops and turns around. "I'll even call Mr. King when we're done and see if I can beg him to let you do your shopping, okay?"

"Sounds good," I squeak, giving him a thumbs-up as I sink back into the driver's seat. Funny that I'm in the driver's seat of my car, isn't it, when I don't even feel like I'm in the driver's seat for my life at the moment.

Zac aside, I've now managed to possibly throw my weekend painting schedule off and added to my to-do list for Monday morning. Plus, the money involved—pay for a new license, pay for a new car registration, and from the looks of things, I'll be paying off a speeding ticket, too.

I gaze out the window, staring at a dust trail a few fields over. Mr. Phoebus must be plowing his fields in preparation for the winter crops they'll be putting in soon. The thought that I know his name makes me smile. That's why I wanted to move to a small town. I wanted to know my local mechanic, shop from the farmers who produce our vegetables, find the local community groups who need help and help them, contribute. I wanted to slow down and enjoy life.

I can feel the tension beginning to release from my neck and shoulders as Zac gets out of his cruiser and starts walking back over to me. Even the sight of a police officer I know walking up to my car, even if he does make me crazy, makes me happy.

However, the look on Zac's face does not make me happy. Not at all.

"Hey, Etta," he says, kneeling down next to the car. "I know you lived in D.C. for a long time, but you would come back and visit, right? Often, too, I'd imagine, huh?"

"Yeah, of course. My grandmother lives here and my

brother, Jack, moved here, so yes. I would visit as often as I could."

"Do you remember getting a speeding ticket on one of those trips down here?"

A nervous flutter begins in the foundation of my gut. I'm not sure I like where this is going.

"Um, yes…I remember one from like four years ago, but I paid for it." Turning my body in the seat so I can face Zac, I feel a cold sweat starting on my hairline. I had paid it, right? "I have a faint recollection of writing a check and putting it in an envelope."

"Would you have kept a record of it?"

"I mean, I can't say for sure, but I can dig into my old bank accounts and find the proof, if that's what you're asking."

Zac bites his lip and stares at me, his eyes almost woeful. Honestly, if I wasn't freaking out on the inside, I would find this kind of lip biting-thing quite sexy, but I'm past that now. We're in a whole other stratosphere, folks.

"Etta," he whispers as he takes a giant gulp of air, "I need you to get out of the car, please."

"Why?"

"Oh man." Zac squeezes his eyes closed as he stands up, reaching his hand behind his back. My heart pounds inside my chest so hard I swear on all things I've ever sworn on that it's going to crack my chest wide open.

"I'm sorry, Etta, but you're under arrest for driving on a suspended license."

EIGHT
Zac

Standing outside her cell, I can't help but think about what just transpired. The ride back to the police station was far from comfortable. Etta remained rigid in the back seat of my cruiser, her shoulders tense and hunched, deliberately avoiding eye contact. Despite my attempts to break the silence and diffuse the heavy tension, all my apologies fell flat.

When we got to the station, protocol took over. I delegated the task of reading Etta her rights to someone else, but I was compelled to assist in processing her arrest—and every moment was painfully excruciating.

Those captivating teal-blue eyes, the ones usually ablaze with a mixture of sass and confidence, now burn with a different intensity: anger and humiliation intermingled. It's a striking contrast to the formidable woman I'm accustomed to dealing with. Yet, deep down, I know her fiery spirit is ever present and waiting to pounce and assert its dominance at any given moment.

I'm not going to lie: it hurts me to see Etta sitting alone like this on the cold metal bench, her back turned to the room.

I approach the bars tentatively. "Hey, Etta, can I get you a glass of water?"

She doesn't turn around. "Are you sure I'm allowed glass in my cell?"

"I'm not positive, but I'm willing to throw caution to the wind this once." When she doesn't bite, I try again. "How about a soda? It comes in its own can; we don't have the fancy glass bottles here."

Silence.

"Come on, Etta, it's not like I arrested you on a felony." I take a chance and step closer to the cell. It is a trepidatious step, but one nonetheless. "I mean, you *could* face up to one hundred and twenty days in jail—"

"Officer Wright, you're not even funny right now." Her shoulders rise and fall as she takes a long breath. "Do you even understand how humiliating this is?"

As much as I hate to admit it, no. I hadn't thought about it that way, from her point of view. I've been too busy worrying about how she was going to react to the fact I was the one bringing her in to even consider how it's making her feel.

I grab a desk chair and roll it over to the cell, sitting down. The Sweetkiss Creek jail isn't big at all; we're a small town. We have three cells in a block off the main office area. The room is a good size and also houses two desks for the two officers who are usually stationed here.

But it's Friday night and everyone is out on patrol. The only person in the cells is...well, I don't need to explain further, do I?

"Don't look at this as embarrassing, Etta, look at it as pure luck."

"Luck." Score. Her body moves, just a smidge. She turns slightly to face me. "How do you see this as luck?"

"Well, it was me who pulled you over. That's one positive thing."

"Wait." Ah ha. More of a turn, now a better angle. I can see her face now with its furrowed eyebrows, extreme irritation, and all the works. "How do you see that as positive?"

"Because it's someone you know pulling you over, not a stranger."

"I'd rather have someone I don't know arresting me, Zac." Annnnd, she turns back around, treating me to a full view of her back again as she returns to staring at the brick wall. "In another town would have been nice, too, so I don't have to have my friend come bail me out while she's at dinner with my other friend, after you, of all people, arrest me."

"It's not that bad," I begin, only to be cut off as someone calls out from the main room. I peek out the door, surprised to see Lt. Brett Simpson from the Lake Lorelei Fire Department standing by my desk.

Glancing at Etta, and seeing her face go white, I can see what she means about being arrested in a different town— Brett works closely with her brother, and you can bet if Brett sees her in that cell, Jack will know she's in here as soon as he leaves. I put my finger to my lips and shake my head, which Etta understands. She sits back in the shadows of the cell and feigns zipping her lips shut.

"Hey, Brett," I say, a bit too jubilant as I walk out of the cell block, closing the door behind me. I course correct and drop my voice down a notch, leaning against a filing cabinet. "What are you doing in my neck of the woods?"

"Hey, Zac." He holds his hand out to pump mine, saying hello. Never mind the confused look on his face as his eyes flick to the shut door behind me. "I just thought I'd stop in to let you guys know I just bought the property that was for sale on the other side of the Sweetkiss Creek Campground woods.

I'll be slowly moving things in over the next month as we get settled in."

I'd met Brett when I moved here and know he's a beloved member of the Lake Lorelei Fire Department. He's a single dad; if he isn't at work, he's at home or with his girl, which makes some of the single ladies around here melt.

"Congrats on the move. I guess we'll be seeing more of you?"

"You will. I'm taking on the captain position at the fire department, starting in two months." He grins, exposing all of his teeth. "That's why we're making the house move happen now. I want to get my daughter settled in her new school and I've got alpacas I need to sort out first, so we're gonna start putting up a fence. But, figured I'd let you guys know in case someone gets twitchy and calls in, trying to say someone's out at the property. If they do, it's me."

"Noted. I'll make sure the other guys know." Chuckling, I shake his hand again as he backs away. "Thanks for stopping in."

As soon as he clears the door and is out of sight, I walk back over to the cell block, opening the door wide. Before walking back inside, I redirect to the station kitchen. I swipe a can of soda from the fridge before heading back to the block and sitting down in my chair again across from Etta.

"So, you're right. It can be that bad." I lean forward, placing the soda on the floor on the other side of the bars. It's like I'm scared of a wild animal.

"Told you." Etta cuts her eyes my way, her gaze leveling on the soda. She gets up and walks over to pick it up. She holds the can aloft. "Thank you. And thank you for getting Brett out of here so fast. If he had seen me..."

"...your brother. I get it. Look, I'll do what I can to keep the gossip at bay. It helps that I'm the only one here right now." I sit back in my chair and pump my hands in the air. "Score one for the small town!"

Etta cracks into her soda can, popping its top and putting the cold liquid to her mouth. She takes a huge sip, wiping her mouth with the back of her hand before focusing on me.

"I should take points away because it's you." She closes her eyes and leans back, banging her head softly against the wall. "I'm leading your team bonding event, but today I'm in your jail?" She then looks at me, her eyes widening. "Oh no, Zac. I needed to get to Mr. King's so I could get the paint supplies I need for tomorrow."

I watch as she sits down and slumps over, putting the can on the floor so she can hold her head with both hands. "I need one thing to go my way."

As if punctuating her thoughts, a ding sounds from my desk in the office beyond. I know it's not my cell phone because mine is in my pocket. A quick glance reminds me I have Etta's phone sitting on my desk still from when we booked her. Her eyes find mine.

"That sounds like my phone. If it is, it's a text and it could be Riley." Her look is pleading. "Will you see if it's her?"

Because I'm a nice guy, I do as I'm told. I cross the space in a few long strides, swiping the phone off my desk. The message flashes on the screen. "It's from…Steve?"

I really didn't think she could slump lower, but yet she does.

She groans. "Can you read it?"

I look back at the screen, which has gone dark. When I touch it, the message pops up, but I need a code or her fingerprint to open the phone. Before I can say anything, Etta is at the cell door, holding her pointer finger high.

"You need this or you can just give me my phone?"

"Can't do that, as much as I want to. I have to follow protocol, Etta." I walk over and let her place her finger on the phone, unlocking the screen. Now I can see the message, so I read it to her. "You're being unreasonable and I'm tired of chasing you. If you won't talk to me in person, and you refuse to speak to me on the phone, you're going to make me do something I don't want to."

The last part of the message sends a sledgehammer to my gut. "What is this, Etta? Who is this guy Steve to talk to you like that?"

"That would be someone who is wrong and who does not get to talk to me." Etta sighs, walking back over to the bench to sit down, facing me. This time she doesn't slump. "Steve is my ex-husband. We're divorced, yet still having irreconcilable differences."

My ears perk up; she has an ex? I'm beginning to see there's more to this woman than meets the eye.

"I had no clue you were married before."

Etta hoists a shoulder, letting it drop. "You never asked."

"True. For the record, I've never been married."

Etta laughs and it's like music. "Good to know. I advise you to think about it before you propose."

"If you don't try out to be St. Valentine in this year's parade..."

"...there's a parade here for Valentine's Day?"

"Oh, come on." I drop my head and cross my eyes, making her laugh again. Now it's like a symphony coming together; the sound is gorgeous. "I'm kidding. I do joke. Maybe too much."

"Maybe." A smile lingers, one side of her mouth upturned as she watches me.

My eyes slam into hers, teal waters coming to life as she stands up and walks across the cell. Like a magnet, I'm pulled from my seat when she does, standing at the same time and meeting her at the bars. Wrapping her hands around the bars, she leans forward, framing her face with the cold steel.

"There's something I have to know," she whispers, smiling coyly.

"Yes?" I whisper back, leaning in so my nose is almost touching the bars myself.

"Why am I not allowed to leave here on my own recognizance and walk home?" she asks, and rather loudly I might add, her voice going up an octave with each word. "Come on, Zac!"

I never get a chance to respond, because as I open my mouth, the front door to the station slams shut, signaling someone's come inside. Looking across the room and into the lobby area, Riley paces, her neck craning, looking for someone to help her. I walk to the doorway and throw my hand in the air.

"Back here, Riley. Come join us."

It only takes her a second to reach us, and when she does, she crosses her arms in front of her chest as she takes in Etta.

"Well, well, well," she says after a good tsk-ing. "And what, pray tell, have you done now, buttercup?"

"I was just asking the good officer why I'm not allowed out on my own," Etta snarls.

"And I was about to let jailbait here know that it doesn't matter if she is the gentlest teddy bear in the world, we have to follow protocol. You get arrested, you get bailed out, and you go to court. The end."

Dragging my eyes away from Etta to Riley, I see real quick she's trying her hardest not to laugh. Riley hands me a slip of paper. "Here, her bond. It was only one hundred dollars, you really couldn't let her..."

I snap a hand in the air. "Zip it." Glancing at the bond, I wave it like a flag. "Let me put this in its file and grab my keys. You'll be out of here in a few minutes."

I walk back out into the main area, leaving them alone. I hear them speaking in low voices as I take care of my own paper trail for work. As soon as I have the paperwork processed, I walk to my desk to snag my keyring and head back to the cell block.

As I get to the door, Riley's voice suddenly drops. Sensing something, I stop at the door. Not meaning to eavesdrop, but doing it anyway, I listen to Etta's strained voice.

"Nothing is going right for me, Riley. Steve's texting more threats. Now I have to look at getting a lawyer to try to prove I paid a fine here a few years ago. And to top it all off, I never made it to King's."

"We can worry about painting your place another time, sweetie. Let's just get you home. I think you need a hot bath and your bed," Riley purrs, making me feel sluggish with the guilt I now carry for having arrested Etta McCoy.

I don't want them to think I've been standing here, even though I have, so I sneak away quietly, back toward my desk. Once I'm there, I start jingling the keys in my clutches loudly. "Found them!"

By the time I walk back over, the women are silent, waiting for me. I pick out a key and put it in the lock only to have it not work. Shaking my head, I fumble around and grab another one, glancing confidently at Etta as I try again. No joy.

Etta rolls her eyes. "Seriously? Now boy wonder can't even get me out of the cell he put me in?"

"Har, har," I manage, struggling to insert another key. Only this time, it works, a satisfying click echoing in the chamber as the door to her cell flies open, releasing Etta back into the world. Riley envelopes her in a hug before she can cross the threshold.

"Well, now you don't have to come over and help me paint tomorrow." Etta pulls away from Riley long enough to stare me down. "Hey, Zac, I'll be home all weekend wishing I could work on my house if you need me or have further need to embarrass me more."

I thought we were on our way to doing better, but it looks like she's got a case of amnesia. "I am really sorry that the timing wasn't right."

"Mmm, do you know anyone who has ever been arrested saying, 'let's do it today, the timing is right?' Because I don't." Etta spins on her heel, linking her arm through Riley's. "Can we go now?"

"Your chariot awaits, m'lady." Riley giggles before turning around to stick her tongue out at me. "Santa is for sure bringing you coal this year."

Etta makes her way across the room with her friend, and my mind spins and swirls. She makes me absolutely insane, but I also feel happy when I see her, like I'm a little boy with butterflies in his stomach on the first day of summer vacation...when you've got the whole summer ahead of you.

But, tossing the little boy's thoughts aside, she also makes my heart slam in my chest at inappropriate times. She makes me smile even though she's a grump—and the fact that she is so grumpy is driving me to want to make her happy.

Only she goes hot, and cold, then hot again...then we're back in the freezer. Who is she and what is this witchcraft she's doing to my heart? She's honestly like a wild horse that needs to be tamed, only that sounds like such a cliché. How about, she's a rabid raccoon? Feral cat?

No, none of that sounds right. She's simply untamed and it's kinda beautiful...in my mind, this could be where my dog training experience could come in handy. Not that she's a dog, but they're cute anyway...

Wow, even my thoughts get panicked when it comes to this woman.

As soon as the front door closes and the pair is gone, I walk back to my desk and sit down, grabbing my phone. I've got two calls to make, but one of them I need to handle now.

I punch in the numbers, and wait for the familiar voice to say hello. When he does, I'm ready.

"Tuck, that bet you talked about, that if I can get Etta to go out with me on a date, you'll give me that baseball card? You're on."

NINE
Etta

Sitting around my living room on this misty Saturday morning was not in the cards. Holding a piping hot cup of coffee, I drop myself into my overstuffed chair, staring out the window and watching droplets slide down the bay window looking out to my front yard.

Glancing around the room, I try to find something I can work on to keep myself busy, only to end up staring at the floor. I really had my heart set on getting this room done today, just to get in a flow with painting this house. It's not like King's Paints is the only business around. There is another big box kind of store about forty-five minutes away I could go to, but by the time I'd get there and come back, I'd lose the time I had set aside this afternoon to work on the final plans and menu for next week's retreat. Conundrum.

An image of Zac Wright sitting in his chair outside of my actual jail cell yesterday is still burned into my mind. I'd come home last night swearing to never speak to him again. Thankfully, my dogs were with the dog walker yesterday, so that was one less thing I didn't have to worry about.

As if they know I'm thinking about them, both boys come

barreling into the room, knocking each other over as they race for the couch. Thor hops up on a pillow that looks out the window, turning in a circle until settling on the perfect position, and Hercules gives up trying to cuddle next to his brother, launching himself off the couch and onto the floor. I watch him burrow a space for himself in his dog bed by the fireplace, closing my eyes as he does.

I must have fallen back asleep for a few minutes, because I'm woken up by a sudden rapping on my front door and by the two dogs who start barking their heads off. Ahhh, my little alarm systems.

I peek through the peephole and almost pass out when I see who it is on the other side.

Keeping the chain lock on the door, I slowly inch my front door open. "Yes?"

Zac cocks his head to one side, rolling his eyes. "You're really not going to open the door the whole way?"

"You could be a burglar. Or here to arrest me again for something else I didn't do." Snapping my fingers, I press my face closer to the opening. "Actually, I stayed up late last night and dug through my old files. I found the canceled check for when I paid my fine, so I think the good people at the Sweetkiss Creek PD may owe me an apology."

"Oh, really?" Zac asks, cracking a smile. "I should come in and verify that for you, and"—he bends over and picks up a giant cardboard box filled with shopping bags—"we could see if I managed to get all the things we need to paint today."

My eyes zero in on one of the bags. It has the giant golden crown with two paint brushes crossed behind it, like a family crest, also known in these parts as the logo for King's Paints.

I close the door, slide the chain off, then open the door wide, stepping back as I do so Zac can enter. Taking a giant breath, he nods his head and starts to put his foot down only to scream and jump back.

"Zac!" My hand flies to my heart as he doubles over. "What's wrong?"

"I'm not sure, but it hurts." He stays bent over for a moment, then slowly rights himself, his face wincing as if he's in pain. "We did that wrong. I'm pretty sure you're supposed to invite the vampire in first, right, as the homeowner?"

When I look at him, his smile bubbles with giddiness and his eyes are filled with laughter. It's like I don't even get a chance to be irritated, because that was funny. Shaking my head, I reach out and grab him by the sleeve and pull him inside.

"Oh, come on. It's rude for me to not ask you to come in now, isn't it?"

As if he knows his bestie is outside, Thor comes racing over to the door as soon as Zac walks in, jumping on his hind legs for attention. Thankfully, Herc stays by my side, watching the whole scene ruefully.

One thing I'd never realized, even though we've been around each other several times now, was how tall and built Zac is. Standing beside what I consider to be my large chair, he makes it look like it belongs in a doll house. Not that I'm small myself, but you know. For a tall girl, it's nice to be able to stand beside a man who is a lot taller than myself.

Zac places the box on my dining room table, pulling out its contents. I recognize all the items I was going to get from King's; it's like he read my mind.

"I feel that look you're giving me," Zac murmurs, a cock-eyed smile playing on his lips. "After you left yesterday, I felt bad, so I called Mr. King at home and asked if he'd open the store for you today. He couldn't, but he did know what you wanted, so he boxed it all up for me to bring over."

My jaw unhinges. Not going to lie. This is one of the nicest things anyone has ever done for me. The fact that it's Zac doing it? I might get my head wrapped around that.

"Wow, he's good." Picking up a pack of drop cloths and a paint tray, I hold them in the air as I chuckle. "These are the exact ones I would have picked out."

"He knows his clientele," Zac muses as he grabs a pack of drop cloths and looks around the room. "So, where do we start?"

I'm sure my face is crinkled with confusion when I look at him. "We?"

"Yep, we." He rips open the bag, pulling out its contents and shaking them. "I figured I'm kind of the reason you weren't able to do this how you wanted to, so how about I come over and help?"

"Okay, well, we're painting this room today." I eyeball him as he starts putting the paint cloths on the floor, second guessing his kindness for wanting something. "Seriously, you don't have to do this. I can do it myself. I'm used to it."

"I'm sure you are used to doing a lot of things by yourself." Zac's green eyes sparkle with amusement. "But, today you don't have to do one of them alone. Okay?"

This goes against all the things I've told myself I would do now that Steve and I are split up. I want to rail against this pushiness, him being here and insisting on helping, yet I'm also tired and part of me feels like if anyone should be here doing this today, it's him.

"I don't see anyone else here offering to help," he continues.

"Only because my helper bailed me out of jail after hours, and she thinks I don't have the supplies I need." I drag my eyes up to meet his again. "I'm sure if I called her and told her I had the supplies now, she'd come."

"Well, she's not here. I am. And if you put on a fresh pot of coffee and get changed outta what must be your pajamas, we can get started." Zac inches closer to me, his smile infectious as he pokes at my middle with his pointer finger.

"Come on, what do you say? Let me help you. Okay? So easy to do."

I look down at my polka dot pajama set and grin.

"Give me five minutes."

Zac isn't half bad at this stuff, I have to say. We spend the better part of the morning getting the first coat up in my living room, only stopping once when I discovered pawprints leading from the painting zone into the kitchen—someone, and I'm not pointing paws, Herc, managed to walk through paint.

Taking a break, I sneak into the kitchen to brew another pot of coffee. A quick glance out the kitchen window into the backyard tells me the rain has stopped, or at least slowed down, the sun now trying her hardest to shine her light through the gray. I find myself fascinated with the shapes of the clouds as the wind blows them across the sky, when Zac clears his throat behind me, causing me to spin around in surprise.

"Sorry, didn't mean to scare you." He points to the coffee pot. "Okay to have a cup now?"

"Of course." I swipe a clean mug from the dish rack, filling it to the brim before sliding it his way. "Help yourself to the creamer."

"I like it black," he says as he toasts me with his mug and takes a sip. Pulling the cup away, he grins again. That same lopsided, sexy smile that he seems to throw out there like he's throwing candy from a parade float. "You make a good cup of coffee."

"Thanks." Filling my cup, I splash a little creamer in it and head out to the living room to survey our work. Feeling the need for music to fill the air, I grab my remote and pull up my playlists, flicking through until I find one from the nineties. I hit play, settling on an old Beastie Boys album.

Tossing the remote back on the couch, I start inspecting the walls as Zac traipses back in, sipping his coffee.

"I would never have pegged you for a Beastie Boys fan."

"Really?" Turning around, I place a hand on my hip and tilt my head to one side. "And what, pray tell, do you think one of their fans looks like?"

"Well, me." He puts his mug down and walks closer to me. "My brother and I used to fight over their albums. We were only allowed to have one album in the family."

Chewing on the inside of my cheek to keep from grinning, I size him up. "What do you mean you were only allowed one?"

"Exactly what I'm saying...we could only have one album. I had to share it with my brother and my sister."

"Ohhh, that's just horrible," I manage with a wink as Zac feigns wiping a tear from his eye and grabs his heart.

"I know. Wretched, right?" He hoists a shoulder in the air, letting it drop. "It was smart of my parents to do really, made us take better care of things and we learned to share."

I'm liking this side of Zac. "Smart parenting."

"I guess so," he starts but is interrupted when his phone chimes from across the room. In a few strides, he reaches it and picks up, reading a text. He taps something back, then places the phone back down and looks at me, his face flushing bright red as he does.

I smell something fishy. "What was that?"

"Well, you're nosy." He shakes his head. "Just cause I feel bad and I'm in your house doesn't mean I'm going to reveal all of my secrets to you."

"Zac." I let the corners of my mouth be pulled up into a flirty smile. "I just watched your face go crimson after you sent that text. You can't come in here and get all embarrassed, then refuse to share what's going on. You saw me in a jail cell yesterday. I think we're past these simplicities."

Zac looks at me, his mouth twitching as he does. "That was my old police department in Beaufort. One of my old friends is retiring, so they asked me to...quilt a blanket for him."

"They—you quilt?" My ears? Can I believe thee? I feel a smile I cannot stop coming; it rises up with laughter, propelling it forward, coming from way down deep within me. Both of my hands fly to my mouth, as if I'm trying to push back in the laugh that escapes. But once I start, I can't stop.

Ever the patient gentleman, as I'm coming to find out, Zac stands and stares at the ceiling, waiting me out. "Okay, yes. Ha ha. Zac quilts. Is it all out of your system now?"

"Okay, wait." I blow out a giant breath, willing myself to be steady as she goes. "Yep, I'm better. But now I want to hear how this happened."

"My grandmother showed me how to do it when I was younger. I was a busy kid, and when my grandfather was governor..."

There's a feeling of cold water being doused on my insides as I realize just what Wright family Zac is from. "Your grandfather was Governor Wright?"

"Yep, the very one." Zac pulls out a chair at the table and sits. "I'd go visit the mansion and get into everything, including meetings I shouldn't be anywhere near. To keep me busy, my grandmother sat me down and taught me to quilt. Every time I came to visit, she made sure to have a project for me. We made small blankets at first, teeny tiny ones. I found out years later we were making them so she could donate them to NICU units all around the state."

My jaw hits the floor with such force, one would think it had broken. Seriously, I'm in such shock that Zac leans over and uses his forefinger to tip my mouth closed again. "I know it's crazy to think you know a man who quilts, but you do."

Shaking my head, I pull a chair out and sit across from him. "I'm a little surprised you're a man who knows his way around some needles, but it's cool. Especially the part where you helped donate what you made for the babies. That's really sweet."

"Eh." Zac shrugs a shoulder, that shade of crimson beginning to drift back onto his features. "I like it. These days, I like making quilts for retirees from public service, which is what the text was about. I get a bag full of fabric and old T-shirts that mean something to the person, usually gathered by a loved one, then they give it to me and I go away and make a quilt for them."

"That's sweet."

"The world is a weird place, so full of sadness and gray. There's some heartbreaking stuff going on out there, and I think that's why I like to be silly and joke. I know it's why I like quilting. I want to remind people there's something good here," he says as he taps his heart. "Good in all of us."

"You are not who I thought you were, Zac. But it's early days still," I say with a wink. Pushing myself back from the table, I stand up and walk around the table, headed toward Zac's side so I can mix more paint and prep to give the room a second coat.

As I do, Zac starts to stand, too, but accidentally kicks the chair beside him, causing it to slide out and clip me on my heel as I go past. It's a direct hit that throws me off course. My balance wanes, and I can feel I'm about to topple to the floor, so I reach out and grab at the only thing within arm's reach: Zac.

I'm aiming to at least clutch at his shirt, but somehow, some way, I manage to grab the band of his sweatpants. Not only am I falling to the floor, but Zac's sweats are coming with me.

He must have felt his pants sliding, because I feel Zac's hand grasp mine, holding everything as stationary as he can around his waist as he flings himself down with me, pulling me on top of him so that we're nose to nose, with two dogs sniffing our foreheads.

I slowly open my eyes, which I had squeezed shut at the end due to the carnage I was about to both witness and partake in, and find a pair of sparkling emerald-green eyes staring back at me.

Zac's eyes crinkle at the corners. "Hi," he whispers, his breath hitting my cheek.

I'd have to be a rock to not feel the chemical reaction that takes over my body at this moment. I could stare at his chiseled jaw and flawless skin for hours, and almost feel the touch of his fingertips ghosting down my side and languidly dragging along the crease of my hips. My hands touch his forearms, and his skin trembles. I feel the rise and fall of his body as he sucks in a breath.

Dragging my eyes to his, I inhale a sandalwood fresh scent as I do. I'm not going to lie: I may abhor this man and dream about torturing him in some fabulous way, but right now, the warmth of his touch and the caress of his fingers as they dance across the back of my arms is beyond thrilling.

Zac slowly sits up, wrapping his arms around me and cradling me as he does, pushing the hair away from my eyes. He thumbs my chin, tipping it toward his mouth, and my breath hitches. Placing my hand on the side of his face, I cup his cheek and raise myself that much closer to him so our noses are barely touching, ever so softly skimming.

KNOCK, KNOCK.

"Yo, Etts, I know you're here. Your car is in the drive."

I'm not sure who moved faster or first, me or Zac, but at

the sound of Riley's voice, we're both up and manage to fly at least six feet apart.

Grabbing my heart, I catch my breath. "Hold on, Riley."

Zac, with his hand on his lips, watches me from across the room. Riley bangs on the door again. "Let me in, woman, I have hot food for you."

Zac motions for me to straighten my shirt, so I tuck it in and check myself in the mirror before flinging open the front door.

"Heeeyyy," Riley says as she peeks over my shoulder, taking in Zac. "Making a house call today? Or maybe you're here to arrest her for something else?"

"Actually," Zac says as he throws an arm in his jacket, "I stopped by to drop a few things off, for penance." He winks. "I need to get going anyway, got the retreat to think about."

He nods at me before excusing himself, squeezing past the two of us standing in the doorway because Riley refuses to budge. She watches him as he walks to his car and climbs in, only turning back to me when he's left the drive.

"Well, well, well," she starts, but I hold up a hand. Do I want to tell my friend I almost made out with the hot police officer who drives me up a wall? No...but yes, cause it's Riley and she knows everything about me.

Riley holds up a white take-out bag. "Orange chicken and peanut noodles. Figured it was a good rainy day lunch meal." She pushes past me, heading for the kitchen. "Wait, do I smell paint?"

"You do," I say with a grin. There's this other part of me that speaks up now and says no, don't tell her. Not yet.

As she disappears out of sight, still chatting away, I allow my fingers to dance on my lips, thinking of what could have been. Glad no one else saw.

Because sometimes, some secrets are more fun kept inside.

TEN
Zac

At one point a few days back, I was looking forward to spending my Sunday going over the proposal for the Canine Comfort Therapy Team. I'm still new here to Sweetkiss Creek, and while I know a few people, I'm not a super outgoing person. I seem like it to most people, but I'm more of a homebody than someone who wants to go out.

But now, parked at the dining room table I share with my absentee and newly married roommate, Reid, I realize today's not a good day to be by myself, cause I'm left alone with my thoughts.

And all I can think about is Etta and her lips.

And that my lips almost touched her lips. Almost.

Honestly, I can only compare the thought of her kiss to a shadow at the end of a summer's day and how it slips away as darkness falls. I know—a little cheesy, a little over the top, but man. This woman is really doing a number to me.

I want to know if she feels like I do...not that I'm even sure what I'm feeling, but I know it's close to crazy. Did she tell Riley, or has she kept it to herself? I imagine if she tells Riley, then next time I see her she'll tease me...or what if she doesn't?

Shaking my head, I want to grab myself by the shoulders and tell me to get ahold of myself. It's like I'm in a trance and it's caused by one woman and her hypnotic lips. For the love of...

I'm still chiding myself when my phone rings. "Hello, Mother, have you had a good weekend?"

"Now that I get to talk to my favorite—"

Another voice pipes in. Seems Mom's on speakerphone.

"Hey," Tuck calls out. "I'm right here. Let's not forget when I showed up at your door with croissants this morning, I was the favorite."

"Oh, sweetie." I can see my mother placating him as if they were sitting here right beside me. Tuck will roll his eyes, and Mom will pat his head lovingly and remind him how smart he is. We obviously have issues and need to be told we're good by our mommy and all the time. "Shut up so I can talk to your brother."

We all laugh as my dad announces himself, too. "Hey, Zac, your mom wants to know if we can crash at your place when we come up for the fundraiser or do we need to book a hotel room?"

I squint, trying to focus on the calendar hanging on the wall across the room. "No, you don't have to get a room. Reid won't be back yet. I'll give you guys my bed, and I'll crash in his."

"What about your brother?" Tuck quizzes me. "I'm wondering where my fiancée and I are going to stay?"

"You can stay—wait." I stand up, kicking my chair back. "Did you say what I think you said?"

"He did!" Mom squeals at an epic pitch in my ear. I think the front glass window on Mr. Payne's house across the street just broke. "We're having a wedding!"

"Tuck, that's awesome, congrats."

"You know there's only one person who can be my best man."

"Have I met him?"

There's a clamor and some commotion as Tuck takes me off speakerphone and presses the phone to his ear. "Okay, you're off speaker. Are you going to do it or what?"

"Be your best man? Of course. It's an honor."

"No, I mean..." His tone is hushed. "Are you bringing Etta?"

"What? I don't know, Tuck." What I do know is that I almost kissed that feral cat yesterday, and I liked it. I can't tell him I don't have a plan. At least not yet. "I plan on asking her out, but you just have to wait and see when it's going to be."

"I told them about her."

"What do you mean, you told 'them?'" A shock blasts through my system. Mom's already in mother-hen-marry-her-kids-off mode, and I'm sure that's heightened now that Tuck's asked Bethany to marry him. "What did you tell them?"

"That there's a girl that lives in the 'crick' who you really like."

"Quit calling it the crick." I sigh. "Someone that lives here, like me, could take offense."

"Stop changing the subject." He drops his voice another octave and whispers, "Are you going to ask Etta or not?"

There's a weird feeling that comes over me when Tuck starts pressuring me like this, and I owe it to that competitive streak we have. I can hear the dare in his voice, taunting me to bring someone, especially now that he's engaged and has someone as his forever. I'd probably feel different about this if I knew he was rooting for me, but I know he isn't. He wants me to show up, alone, explaining to my parents why this woman wouldn't come to the dance with me. It's starting to feel like high school.

There's also the perspective where he doesn't want to part

with that baseball card as much as I don't want to lose it. So. Yeah. There's that.

Tuck clears his throat. "If you don't ask, no baseball card."

I stare at the calendar on the wall. Do I want to ask her to the fundraiser? Yes, but it's in less than two weeks. I'm questioning my skills to win Etta over. "You realize we sound like little kids, right?"

"Spoiled ones at that," my mother sings out. Great, I'm back on speakerphone. Would have been nice to have been warned. "Fighting over a baseball card. But, Tuck says this woman you're bringing is very nice."

"Is that right, Zac?" my dad pipes in. "Should we all go to dinner before..."

"No, I'm sure she's busy." Looking around me, I'm frantic. I want to get off this call. I don't like lying to my parents, and I don't want to murder Tuck over the phone. None of this is ideal at the moment, and I just want to finish my work.

Seeing the stack of papers in front of me, I do the unthinkable. I grab a few sheets, crumpling them close to the speaker of my cell, mimicking what hope sounds like static. "I...what's...can't...hear...you."

There's a brief pause, and I wonder if they're all in the car looking at each other and questioning my sanity before my mother speaks up.

"Honey? Are you still there? Tuck, call him back. It sounds like we lost him."

"I'm sure he's there," Tuck says with a Southern drawl, his accent thick today.

"I can't believe..." I let the crumpling commence, pressing it harder into the phone. "...you...think..."

"We'll try you when we get home, Zac," Dad commands, probably cutting his eyes at Tuck right now, if I know him.

"Dad." Tuck's voice is exasperated. "I'm telling you, he's not—"

And the line goes dead. Hallelujah.

Placing my phone down on the table, I head into the kitchen to make another pot of coffee. As I lean against the counter, waiting for it to do its thing, I start to second-guess the whole bet with Tuck. I mean, after yesterday at her place, how could I not question myself?

If someone had asked me a few weeks ago about Etta, I would have laughed and told them she's like olive oil to my water. But today? Today, she's the jelly that goes with my peanut butter sandwich. She's sugar I'd like to add to my tea. She is the ham that is meant for my burger.

You get my drift.

Etta McCoy has somehow managed to reach inside me and wrap her fingers around my heart, and I don't want her to let it go. The thing is, I'm not sure she even realizes she's done it.

And I arrested her.

Reaching into the cabinet above the coffeemaker, I grab a fresh mug. I'm still shaking my head as I fill the mug and take a sip, setting it down slowly before I bring my palm to my forehead and smack myself. If we do go out and I'm lucky enough that we last, it's going to be a great story:

So how did you two meet?

Well, I kinda knew her, then I arrested her...

I make my way back into the dining room, grabbing the stack of papers and heading to the couch for a change of scenery. I glance at my watch; I've got another hour allotted to finish this up for its submission, then I need to pack for the retreat in two days.

My heart literally skips a giant beat when I think about it. Two days at the campground working with my enemy-friend. Or is she now my friend-enemy?

Whatever she is, I'm here to figure it out.

ELEVEN
Etta

While going to the local department of motor vehicles to update my car registration surprisingly wasn't a chore and didn't even take that long, my stop to pick up food from the local grocer is turning out to be the exact opposite.

Mitchell, the owner of Buttar's Grocers, and his wife, Livvy, are honestly the best ever. Their small store caters to locals and tourists alike, so they constantly like to keep new products on the shelves, rotating them so they supply what's on trend as well as stocking all the old favorites. Thankfully, they have their finger on the pulse for food allergies, too—Livvy, who is finishing off the last of the list, holds up a few boxes of gluten-free cookies and waves them in the air for me.

"I tried these the other day. Not bad. Definitely don't taste like cardboard." She winks as she slides them into the box. "Now, I think we have one last box of gluten-free cinnamon-sugar graham crackers. Pretty sure I put them to the side the other day when the order came in. Let me check in the back."

Mitchell waits for her to leave the room before he turns to me and grins, holding a finger to his mouth. "Shhh, don't tell her, but I ate the graham crackers. And I'm not even gluten free."

Chuckling, I grab some produce and add it to the pile in front of me. "I'm sure no one will miss them."

My phone goes off in my bag. Thrusting my hand inside, I pull my phone out and see Amelia's name flashing on the screen. I hold the phone up as I duck out the front door. "Be back in a minute; it's the boss calling."

Mitchell nods as I close the door behind me and press the phone to my ear. "Yes, boss?"

"Don't call me that; it's just weird." Amelia laughs. "You almost done at the store?"

"I am. By the time we hang up, I should be able to pay and get outta here. I already went to the DMV, so I'm on-site the rest of the day setting up."

"Oh, thank goodness." Amelia lets out a sigh of relief in my ear. "I'm actually calling because I realized something last night. Without Dylan here, I don't have anyone to stay overnight and act as the camp manager. So there's no one around if something goes wrong—not that it will."

"Oh, great, you know you just Murphy's Lawed us, right?"

"Stop being such a ninny. I don't believe in that stuff, but I do believe in my guests feeling like they're taken care of. Do you mind staying here tomorrow night with the group?"

Do I mind? Part of me wants to admit that I do mind, both because it's not my home and Zac will be here. The other part of me wants to admit that I'd love to stay overnight... because it's camp. And Zac will be here.

I'm pretty surprised when I catch myself saying that last sentence in my mind. Have I been stuck thinking about what it would have been like to have kissed Zac Wright the other day? Oh yes. Willingly, I have stayed levitating in an almost dreamlike state thinking of the warmth of his skin and the heat of his breath on my cheek. His scent was clean and fresh, like a load of washing hung outside on an August afternoon in the sunshine blowing in a gentle breeze.

"Etta." Amelia's voice, more rushed than usual, cuts through the fog of my thinking. "Is it cool? Will you stay over? Don't worry, you'll get paid for the time, too."

"Of course I can do it. No problem at all." Then two little figures pop to mind. "I need to figure out where the dogs can stay, though."

"I'll take care of it and pay for your dog sitter, so do what you have to, okay?"

I can't tell from her voice if Amelia's irritated, because she sounds like she's in a hurry, or if she's being generous. I'm thinking she's irritated with something, but no need to bring it up now. There are a lot of things she could be stressed about, and I'm not going to add to it and bug her.

"Anything for you." I mean it, and she knows it. I hear it reflected in her voice when she responds.

"Thank you," she whispers. "I'll touch base later."

After we disconnect, I walk back inside to Buttar's to pay for everything, and Mitchell and Livvy help me load up my tiny VW with all the supplies. Once we're done, I hop behind the wheel of my car and pull out of the parking lot.

It takes about eight minutes to get from the store to the campground. I even check the clock on my phone when I pull up to make sure. Patting myself on the back for a productive morning, I grab my keys so I can unlock the kitchen and put the food away.

As I flick through the bevy of keys on my ring to find the one I need to open the door, I find myself thinking strange thoughts...like, I wonder if Zac is the one who's gluten free? Poor guy...if it is him, I know how much he's looking forward to those s'mores, so he's going to be disappointed when he finds out he doesn't have any graham crackers to go with it.

And why on earth am I thinking about Zac? Shaking my head as if to toss the thought out, I get down to business.

I manage to unload a few boxes before my phone beeps, signaling a text. Grinning, because I'm certain it's Amelia with more items to add to my to-do list, I swipe the phone from my back pocket only to go limp when I see who it is.

STEVE: *I want to talk. I think we'll get more accomplished if we meet in person. Are you free if I come down this week?*

ME: *No. There's nothing to say.*

STEVE: *I just want to talk.*

I wish I could believe him, but I think it's fair to say my trust switch has been flipped off at the moment. Taking my own energy temperature, I decide it's fairly lower than I'd like it to be, so I do what my old therapist used to encourage me to do with Steve: I disengage.

I start to slide my phone back into my pocket, but instead I turn the ringer off and go put it in my car. The only person I need to talk to today is Amelia, and she knows where I am.

Once I've got everything unloaded, I grab the folder for the retreat off Amelia's desk and double-check our confirmed attendees. We've got a group of twelve, including Zac, so I grab the housing map so I can note who will sleep where.

Opening the folder, I'm surprised when a sticky note falls into my lap. Picking it up, I scan it, reading it not once but twice because my eyes cannot believe what I'm seeing.

On the map in front of me, Amelia has placed a giant red X across the bunk rooms, the place where I thought we'd be putting everyone. However, according to the note I'm reading, she's changed things.

Hey E, I'm so sorry but Spencer accidentally booked workmen to start updating the bunkhouse...tomorrow. I've allocated the cabins for everyone to use, there will be plenty of room for up to four people in each. Hopefully, that means you'll get a cabin all to yourself :) so stake your claim, sister! Thanks again, A. xx

I let the note drop from my grasp, floating back onto the paperwork in the folder. At least she left me with a good solution and I still get a room by myself. I honestly don't think I could imagine sharing with anyone right now, not with the mood swings I get lately.

"Hello?"

Jumping in the air and almost out of my skin, I dash over to the window to see who called out. Standing by a truck filled with a few suitcases and some more supplies is Zac.

Spying me at the window, he puts his hand up to his forehead, shielding his eyes from the sun, and waves in my direction. I unlock the window and slide it up, sticking my head out.

"Can you come down and let me in? The door's locked."

"It's locked to keep the riffraff out."

He cocks his head to one side. "I'm not riffraff, I'm all the man that you need."

I step back and point a finger at him. I'm not sure Ms. Houston would be impressed with his use of her lyrics. "Stay there, I'll be right down."

As I make my way back downstairs, my heart starts this tip-tapping thing, excited. It's so unnerving, I stop at the bottom of the steps and wait for a moment, checking to see if it's fluttering and making sure I'm not having some kind of "episode" as my grandma would call it.

I stand at the bottom of the steps, my right hand on my heart as it pounds *paTHUMP*, *paTHUMP*, echoing inside my rib cage. It feels like a normal beat until I glance up and see Zac with his face pressed to the glass so his right side is smooshed against it, grinning at me and tapping on the window.

"Let me in. Please?"

My heart feels like it could explode it's pounding at such a rapid pace. And I think it's all because of—him?

Shaking my head, I step backward up the flight of stairs so I'm out of view. Am I becoming attracted to Zac Wright? I mean, I guess I could be, but...do I want to be? That's the question, and it seems—from the perspiration slick on my palms—I suddenly care more than even I knew I could.

"Get it together, woman," I mutter to myself. Squaring my shoulders, I take a giant breath of air. I can be professional and I will be professional.

Holding my head high, I put my foot out to take a step... only I forget I'm one stair above the actual first floor. Do I fall and crumble into a giant pile of withering insanity, wishing I could disappear before my hands smack on the floor in my mad effort to catch myself?

Oh, you bet I do.

I look up to find Zac with a look on his face that is an equal mix of both horrified and hysterical. I can tell he's trying to swallow his laughter as he points to me and then back at himself.

"I'd help you if I could get inside," he screams.

"I'm not in some chamber where you need to yell," I scream back. "I can hear you—the windows are only single glazed."

Grabbing at the railing, I pull myself up into a standing position and ignore the man-child with his face still pressed against the window. I walk over and unlock the door, turning away after I do.

"You can come in now," I call out over my shoulder. Feeling something warm in the palm of my hand, I look down half expecting it to be dripping with even more perspiration, but it's not that—my hand is bleeding.

Zac is closing the door behind him when I groan.

"What's wrong now?" His arms are filled as he hauls a few

bags inside by himself, walking them over to one of the dining room tables. Pain in my hand aside, those are some sculpted biceps on that man, and for real, there is nothing I find sexier than the curve of a man's bicep.

"I've cut myself." I hold my hand up and point to the scratch, which for such a tiny thing is bleeding profusely. "Must have gotten caught on a splinter when I fell."

"I hope you have good insurance, Calamity Etta." Zac winks as he crosses the room and holds out his hand. "Let me see."

Placing my hand in his, I can't help but notice how close we're standing. There's that scent of his again. I'm not sure what it is he's splashing on his skin, but it's not Etta repellant, I can tell you that much.

Calming myself, I watch as he inspects my hand. Still holding my hand in his, he looks at me, his eyes' usual emerald green have turned almost jade in color.

"Do you have a first aid kit?"

I can feel the color drain from my face. "Is it that bad?"

"No." He chuckles. "We need to disinfect it and get a Band-Aid."

"Oh." Crisis averted, I let my shoulders drop from where they'd hiked to my ears and dip my chin in the direction of a cabinet across the room. "Amelia keeps it in there."

Zac lets go of my hand, my skin feeling a chill where his warmth once was when he does. Opening the cabinet door, he rustles around inside for only a moment before he turns around victorious.

"Found 'em." He holds up some bandages and a roll of tape in the other. He nods his head toward the kitchen. "Let's do this over the sink."

"Seriously, I can do this myself," I start to object, but then follow him into the next room. "It's embarrassing enough you witnessed my fall, but now you're cleaning up the carnage, too."

We've stopped at the sink, Zac leaning against the counter. He runs the tap water and takes my hand in his again. "Shush. I'll do this for you, then I have to go back to work."

The quiet in the room is thicker than a bowl of gravy. You know the kind of quiet I'm talking about: when you feel that all of the air you could be breathing has left your system and you recognize that you're standing still for a moment in time. Granted, this is an embarrassing moment for me, but a moment nonetheless.

While Zac's busy rinsing my hand, I study him. I let my eyes drag along his jawline and skim his neck, reminded it wasn't long ago we were thisclose together and thisclose to kissing. Allowing my gaze to dance across his chest, I'm starting to get it. I can only imagine this man has had women throwing themselves at him for years. Even if he is a quilter.

Hmmm. Quilting. I don't know a lot about that, just that there's binding, and sashing, there's applique, ornamental needlework, and tacking. And I only know this much because of course I looked it up on Mr. Google after Zac left the other day. I could use a good tacking myself...

"Does that sting?" Zac's voice drips with worry, a nice look on him if I do say so myself.

I start to shake my head from side to side, when a piercing sting begins to rise from my tiny wound. "Oh, yeah, actually. Ow!"

"Sorry," he whispers, taking my hand and lifting it to his lips. My breath hitches as his lips brush across my skin, sending a thousand tiny ripples of electricity across my flesh. My breath is crippled. I'm starting to worry I'm going to need more resuscitation myself.

Zac lets his lips linger on my skin for another moment before he pulls away, a dangerous smile playing on his lips as he gently dries my wet hand with a clean towel. "Is that better?"

I want to pull my eyes from his, but I can't. I can only nod and fight the shaking and shuddering that my body wants to do.

He places the bandage on my skin, fastening some tape down over it. He holds his hands over the wound, his warmth surrounding my hand.

"Thank you," I manage, finally getting the nerve to move my eyes away from his. The room feels thick again, but this time it's awkward. Overwhelming? Surprising.

And confusing. So, so confusing.

"Okay, well, I need to finish unloading and get back to the station." Zac claps his hands together and points to the front door. "I'll be out of your hair in a few minutes."

I stay standing at the sink while Zac goes back to his purpose for being here. From my vantage point, I watch him as he gathers a few more bags from his truck and does a careful balancing act to bring them all inside. The heat which had been building inside me is finally calming down, like a fire that has gotten a good dousing.

Inhaling a giant breath of air, I close my eyes and steady myself as that unpredictable flutter in my chest comes rippling back. I can't ignore the sparks between us, and I think it's because I don't want to.

A weird acid feeling hits my stomach as I realize what's happening.

I'm falling for Zac Wright.

TWELVE

Zac

This morning has flown by, and no wonder—I've been going a mile a minute since I woke up today. My alarm had buzzed at six and I was out the door on my morning run by five minutes past, back by seven for a quick shower and breakfast before I had to go. I was happy I'd dropped all my things off yesterday because it made it that much easier to get out the door so I can be here on-site at the campground by eight. The team won't start arriving until after nine, but at least I'm here if needed.

Etta has set up a check-in table in the dining room and put out trays of snacks. There's a large silver container filled with ice and stuffed with cans of soda and Cheerwine, and a bevy of small brown bags in which she's packed a lunch for each retreat-goer to take with them as they check into their cabins.

"You really thought of everything to welcome us here, didn't you?" I ask as I spin around and look at the whole setup. "You should run your own hotel."

"I just did things how I'd like them to be if it was my team event, you know?" She walks over and stands next to me with a bunch of freshly picked lavender in her hand. "When I was running my old business, the winery, I used to pay attention to the little details our customers asked for, and then I'd replicate it for other events." She holds the bunch of lavender aloft in one hand, and in the other, she shows off a ball of twine. "Like this."

She holds out the ball of twine, indicating for me to take it, so I do. "What's this for?"

"Well, you're going to tie a string of twine around each bag, and we'll stick one or two pieces of lavender in the bow. It adds a little flair."

My right eyebrow hikes itself up to the top of my forehead. Don't ask how, it's a gift handed down to me from my father. "It adds flair, does it?"

A flash of pink flushes her cheeks—it's coupled with a tiny grin she tries to hide from me and it sends a thrill to my very core. What is it about this woman that makes me want to see her smile all the time?

I take the twine, grab a pair of scissors, and point to the bags, trying to push away the memory of my lips on her hand just yesterday in this very room. "Should I start now?"

"Please. The retreat is over tomorrow, so we need to hurry," she teases. I could get used to this Etta. I wonder if she could get used to me?

We work in silence, with me snipping twine and tying it around the lunch bags and Etta following me, shoving pieces of lavender through the bows. My palms are sweaty, to the point that if I had on khakis and wanted to wipe them on my pants, there's no way I could without being busted for wet hands. There's no doubt in my mind this woman makes me sweat in the best way possible…if there is a good way to sweat, that is.

Out of the corner of my eye, I watch Etta as she snips the

lavender in her hands and finishes stuffing its flowers into the last bow before she steps away with a smile. "They look pretty, don't they?"

"Yes," I acknowledge, but I'm not looking at the lunch bags.

Etta's eyes zip to mine as the door from outside swings open. A woman I recognize, with long blonde hair pulled back into a secure ponytail, peeks her head inside and calls out. "Is this where I sign up for the adult camp?"

"Lucy Bothalmey, it's good to have you," I say, ticking her name off the sign-in sheet. "First one here, huh?"

Lucy's eyes trip around the space, taking it all in as she nods her head. "Kinda. Parker and Miller pulled up at the same time I did, but they're still outside."

Next to me, Etta clears her throat as she reaches across me with her hand out. "Hi, Lucy, I'm Etta. Welcome to the Sweetkiss Creek Campground."

"Oh." Lucy's eyes start at Etta's feet and make their way up in the most obvious sizing up I've ever been a witness to. "Who are you?"

"I work here. If you need anything at all, just let me know," Etta says, her phone beeping in her hand. She glances at the screen, rolls her eyes, then puts her hand down. "I'm on-site for the duration of your stay."

"Mmmm." Lucy nods her head sharply, her lips pressed in a thin line that slowly begins to turn up at the corners. "Honestly, if I need anything, I'll ask our camp counselor." Her charcoal-lined blue eyes sparkle as she turns her attention to me, reaching out to grasp my bicep. "And that's you, correct, Wright?"

Her hand lingers a moment too long, so I step back, feeling uncomfortable, letting her hand drop back to its natural place at her side. Lucy's nice enough, but she's made no bones about how she feels about me from the moment I started. Sergeant Lane had pulled me aside my first day to let me know she'd requested to work with me as my partner, but he'd told her no.

I start to say something, but I'm interrupted by Etta's phone dinging again. Looking her way, I wait for her to check her phone, but instead she just looks at me as it goes off again. When it goes off a third time, she glances at it and huffs, dropping her hand again.

"Etta is my co-counselor, if we're putting things in terms of camp, Lucy." I nudge a surprisingly rigid Etta gently with my elbow. "Wouldn't that be the best way to put it?"

"I think so," she replies through gritted teeth, forcing a smile. Etta then reaches for a brown bag lunch and swipes it, tossing it to me as she walks away waving her phone in the air. "Here, give this to Lucy. I need to handle this. I'll be back in a sec."

It's with a tiny jolt of fear that I watch as Etta disappears into the kitchen, tapping away on her phone as if she's texting for her life. Beside me, Lucy—who is reading over her retreat agenda—takes her hip and checks mine, winking at me.

"So, did you do the cabin arrangements?" she asks, pointing to a map I hadn't seen yet. The map is a drawing of the campground and shows what buildings are what, where the boat launch and dock is, and there's a section where the cabins are mapped out. Someone had listed our names beside each cabin.

When I look where Lucy points, my stomach dips. Oh, no no no. Whoever made the bed arrangements has put us in the same cabin. I scan the list quickly to see if there's anyone else I can swap places with. I decided to bide my time and find someone later in the day.

As I turn to answer Lucy, I'm thrilled when Parker and Miller come barreling inside, hands in the air, singing "The Final Countdown" and laughing. Looking beyond them, I can see a few more cars driving single file up the lane, one after the other. Within a few minutes even Etta's back by my side, and we're ready—signing everyone in, giving them agendas, and sending them off to their cabins to unpack.

Let the games begin.

"Okay, you guys, I think everyone's here." I look around the room and count twelve heads, including me. "Yep, we're all here. So we're going to start with an icebreaker to get everyone playing together, sound good?"

Lucky for me, this crew is into the whole team bonding thing, and they all cheer when I ask. "You guys are an easy crowd. Okay, Miller, come on up."

Etta had briefed me on an improv game she always played with her employees called Zip, Zap, Zop. "I'm going to show you all how to do this with Miller, then I want everyone to come up and do it for a couple of rounds."

I quickly explain the game, still marveling at its ease and how quickly it can become comical. "The leader, in this case it'll be Miller, starts with a 'Zip' and passes it to the person either to the left or right—when I say pass, you're pretending the word is like a ball. It's up to the person who receives it which direction to pass it, and they will say 'Zap' when they pass it. The next person must 'Zop' it, sending it to someone across the circle. 'Zip' and 'Zap' can only be sent to either your left or right...and I want all of you to say the words in your best Italian accent."

No one moves, so I clap my hands together. "Come on, people, let's go!"

As everyone scrambles, laughing and getting into a circle, I head into the kitchen to see if there's any kind of prep I can help Etta with. She'd been tasked with coordinating our dinner, and I don't want her to be overwhelmed.

When I don't find Etta in the kitchen, I jog to the back pantry and whip the door open. I'm in such a rush I don't see her as she's coming out of the pantry with her arms full. Our bodies slam together, comically, with Etta grunting as she smacks into my chest.

"Hey." She half laughs, catching a bag of pasta as it starts to tumble from her arms. "Watch where you're going."

"Sorry about that." Steadying us, I grab her elbows and pull her close to me. "You okay?"

She takes a step away and cocks her head to one side. "Are you looking for excuses to get close to me, Zac Wright?"

Is this Etta being flirty with me? I need to start calling this Etta our Camp Counselor Etta. She's fiery, and flirty, and a lot of fun.

I cock my head to one side, mimicking her pose. "And what if I am?"

I take a step closer and catch a whiff of flowers. Lavender. My lavender girl.

She giggles as she clears her throat and licks her lips before dragging her eyes to meet mine. "Well." She holds up her arms, showing me how full they are. "It's not like I can fight you off, now, is it?"

This game we're playing is delicious. I'm about to go all in, when someone calls out, "Anyone back here? Hello, Etta?"

Etta all but flings herself out of the pantry. "Oh, hey, Brett. What are you doing here?"

Realizing it's Lieutenant Brett from Lake Lorelei fire company, I quickly straighten my shirt and make sure it's tucked in and I'm not looking like I'm a giant mess as I roll out of the pantry...that I was just crammed in with Brett's boss's little sister. Man, things can get complicated in a small town.

Seeing some boxes of food on the floor of the pantry, I grab a few things to make it look like I'm supposed to be there.

When I step out of the pantry, Brett's eyes slam into mine and he cocks his head to one side. Grinning, I hold up a bag of sugar and a tub of...prunes.

"It's not a party until the prunes come out," I manage.

"Yeah, that's just weird, Wright." Brett looks at me like I've got snakes for hair, then his expression changes. He snaps his fingers together. "Oh, that's right. You guys are here for your team bonding, aren't you? Sorry to interrupt."

"It's fine," Etta says, leaning against a counter. "What's up?"

"Well, I'm not sure if you know, but I've moved into the small farm on the other side of the Lorelei Woods, so our properties border each other. My alpacas are being delivered in an hour, but we just found a giant hole in the fence."

"Oh, man," Etta sympathizes. "That stinks."

"It does, but luckily when I called Amelia and asked if you guys have any space, she said I could use the fenced area behind Dylan's cabin." He looks pleadingly at Etta. "She mentioned the latch was funny but said you'd show me how it works."

"Totally." Etta doesn't need to be asked twice; she's already one foot out the door. "Follow me."

"Oh, wow." Brett's pinched face softens. "Thank you so much. I don't know what I would have done with Chewpaca and Tupaca if I didn't find a place to put them today."

"Chewpaca...and Tupaca?" Pure joy shines as her smile swings free. "You're going to need to tell me the story behind those names, Brett."

Watching Etta and Brett trot away, laughing, I realize I love seeing her smile. I love being the person who makes her smile, and I want to see it more and all the time. It's like her laugh. It's a laugh that when I hear it, I'm in on the joke with her.

And I don't feel corny when I think it's music to my ears, because it really is.

She's an earthworm, burrowing inside my heart. My little lavender earthworm.

I'm going to need to work on that nickname.

THIRTEEN

Etta

I've spent the last couple of hours keeping my eyes on Lucy. I know, I shouldn't even be feeling like I need to watch her, but I do. I watch her while she watches Zac. It's becoming a thing.

This morning, we'd handed out blue flags and red flags for them to tie to their clothing so we could separate them into teams. I'd watched Lucy as she sidled up to Zac, holding out her flag and asking him to tie it on her wrist.

Did I roll my eyes so hard it hurt? I did. I wanted to grab her by her ponytail then whisper in her ear, "I'm the one who almost kissed him, not you, *Lucy*."

The one good thing to come out of the morning is that my aunt's next door neighbor called me. Another perk of living in a small town: when you need a lawyer you can find one easily. My brother had recommended I call this person and, luckily for me, John was able to take my case.

Had I glared at Zac the whole time I spoke to John? You bet I did—in between the moments I wasn't feeling his breath still on my cheek or his lips on the palm of my hand, that is.

Glancing out the giant window that overlooks the lawn all

the way to the lakeside, I can see the teams starting to split up. They've been outside doing some kind of three-legged-race-relay-tug-of-rope thing, but now I watch as everyone breaks and heads down to the lakeshore taking their brown bag lunches with them, minus Zac. Spotting me at the window, he holds up a finger asking me to wait a sec and sprints my way.

"Here," he says as he runs inside and grabs a cardboard box by the front door with reams of colored stock paper inside. "I know it's a literal rainbow in there, but I wanted this to be colorful."

Taking it from him, I place it on the counter beside me and cock my head to one side quizzically. "Am I making origami?"

"Sometimes I can't tell if you're being serious or kidding," he says, eyeing me. "You tend to use a touch of sarcasm to highlight your sentences when you speak to me."

A little tiny tug happens in my tummy. It's not the first time I've been told I have a sarcastic edge. "Really? Do I come off a little too hard?"

Zac adjusts the blue flag on his belt loop as he tilts his head to one side and looks at me, a tiny smile twitching at the corners of his mouth. "Are you worried?"

"I mean...well, yes." I feel my cheeks flush hot with heat. "I've been told my tone can be biting, and I try to keep a lid on Esther, but she's my defense mechanism."

"Esther?" Zac's mouth swings open. "Who are you talking about?"

"My other personality," I sigh, pulling out a selection of red, orange, yellow, and green paper. "I don't know how to explain it. Esther shows up when I'm in defense mode; she's a little bit short with her temper and not one to suffer fools."

"What makes you be so defensive?"

"Well, not sure if you're aware, but I was arrested recently..."

He grimaces. "I'm really sorry about that."

"Hey, the DMV let me keep my license since the ticket has been paid. My lawyer has already spoken to the judge, says the charges will be dismissed and I won't have to go to court." I look pointedly at Zac. "However, since I spent most of the day in jail, my lawyer thinks it would serve you right to have to pay me for my time that day."

"I was doing my job, Etta. Come on, silver looks good on you," Zac teases me.

"I'm a law-abiding citizen, Zac Wright. I err on this side of Lady Justice....and yes, I know silver looks good on me, thank you."

Glancing up at him, I find Zac watching me with this look on his face. His eyes search mine, and I feel my insides dip. I'm revealing more than I want to. Scolding myself, I bite my tongue—next thing you know I'll be sharing my social security number with the guy.

Covering my nervousness, I grab at the cardboard box, thrusting it between us.

"So, what are my instructions?"

"This little ditty is my favorite—it's called Random Acts of Kindness."

I hold up a piece of paper. "Are we writing random acts of kindness on these?"

He shakes his head no. "Everyone has to write something nice about someone else who's here. I've put everyone's name in a hat, which we'll pass around and have everyone pull out a slip of paper. The name they get is the person they have to write nice things about."

"That's a good idea. I take it you want me to cut these pieces of paper in half?" Zac nods, and I grab the scissors. "How many sheets do I need to cut in half?"

"Not many, I overdid it on the paper." He shrugs. "I figure I'll donate it to the local school after we're done."

"Do-gooder," I tease.

"Esther the patience tester," he teases back.

"Not that I'm complaining about the games you're doing, but why don't you have more competition style games lined up? I think I saw on the agenda that the relay you did this morning is the only one."

"Well," Zac begins, clearing his throat. "I did that on purpose. I didn't want to have too many events that required winning. It can be disappointing if you're not the winner and it can cause rivalry that we don't need on a team retreat."

"Fair point, but you're all adults. I'm sure you can keep it friendly."

"Actually..." Zac sighs, turning his head slightly toward mine. "It was more designed this way so *I* wouldn't get uber-competitive and try to win everything."

"Wait—you?" Stepping back, I look him up and down. Not bad, not bad at all, but I fight my face from letting it show my pleasure. "Okay, you could win a race, I'm sure..."

"See, don't do that." Zac cracks up, poking my side with his finger. "It's tormenting and taunting that gets me riled up. I'm not sure why, but I can go from zero to one-eighty in a matter of two seconds when it comes to competing." Emerald green eyes flash my way. "I blame my brother."

"Trauma always seems to come from a sibling. Younger brother?"

Zac nods. "He's perfect. He's followed the path my mom wanted him to; he's a lawyer, and man, he's good at it."

"My sibling is my twin, so you don't have to tell me about trauma. I spent my childhood trying to form my own identity and then my teens trying to get out from under his shadow."

Zac attempts to bite back a grin. "And now as an adult, you move to the town over from where he lives..."

"I know, it's crazy-making, but I guess I'll spend my adulthood trying to be the best sister I can be to him and his wife. I daydream about taking care of their kids." Laughing, I take all of the half-pieces of paper and straighten them into a pile, handing them off to Zac. "Here. You're ready for your random acts."

"Thanks." Zac reaches out for them and his hand touches mine, faltering for a moment. Frozen, I'm not moving as he strokes his finger over my wrist. Taking a deep breath, I raise my eyes to his. He opens his mouth to say something, only to be interrupted.

"Etta, do you have any trash bags? We need something for our lunch sacks and leftovers."

My back is to the door, but I don't have to turn around to know the voice. "We do, Lucy, in fact I put one in the trash can down by the lake earlier." Tightening the smile on my face, I indicate beyond the window to the giant metal trash can by the picnic table on the lake shore.

"Oh, my," she manages with her sweet, Southern drawl sounding like she's added sugar to it. "I swear, I looked around and didn't see it!"

"Well, that's not a good trait for a police officer to admit." Meaning to mumble it under my breath, I think we're all shocked when I say these words out loud. Lucy's eyes widen and swirl with storm clouds, and Zac literally bites his bottom lip, his eyes wide as saucers.

I need to fix this. "I mean, you know, if you were trying to collect evidence and you miss something, you don't want to admit that you looked around and just 'didn't see it,' right?"

My mother used to call my attempts at overcorrecting myself the greatest blunder ever. Nine times out of ten, me trying to make a situation better, I can make it worse. A point I'm proving right now.

"You know, Lucy, we're about to do a new task." Zac to the rescue. He hands her the paper. "Can you carry this down to the picnic table for me?"

"Of course." She cuts her eyes my way as she takes the papers from Zac. She turns to go, but spins around and puts her hand on his arm. "Do we need to be in teams or paired up for this?" she asks, voice hopeful.

"Nope, no pairing up." Zac's a bit too cheerful as he delivers the disappointing news. Walking beside her, he throws a smile over his shoulder my way as they wander down to the lake.

A commotion out of the corner of my eye pulls my gaze from the two of them over to Dylan's house. When I look, there's nothing there, so I pull my eyes away and go back to staring at the back of Lucy's head. That's when a flash of something draws my attention back to Dylan's.

Squinting my eyes, I look closer. When I do, my eyebrows lift in surprise all the way to my hairline. I'm no animal expert, but that looks like an alpaca walking around the outside of Dylan's house toward me. On further inspection, I see that yes —we have one alpaca safely in the fenced-in area, but another one is wandering freely, eating Dylan's front lawn.

Thankfully, I have Brett's number on my phone. Pulling it up, I shoot him a quick text that one of his babies has gotten out before shoving the phone back into my pocket and heading out the door. I've never had to wrangle an alpaca before. How hard can it be?

As I make my way to Dylan's, the alpaca freezes when he sees me coming. Stopping for a moment, I give it a second to make sure this animal isn't going to charge me before I take a few more steps. The alpaca looks at me and walks straight toward me, which surprises me. We make eye contact for a moment before it suddenly pivots and changes direction, walking at a fast clip which turns into a light jog as it heads toward the lakefront.

When I follow the path in its trajectory, I can see only one obstacle in its way. Well, two really, and this won't be pretty if they collide. The alpaca is picking up speed, now headed straight for Zac and Lucy.

Horrified, I do the only thing I can think of: I start screaming and running in the opposite direction of Lucy and Zac, waving my hands wildly in the air, hoping I steal the animal's attention.

I hear the thudding of hooves on the ground behind me, telling me I've done my job well, and I swear to the heavens I've never in my life run this fast before. This is the kind of fast I think a perp would go when trying to get away from the cops, or maybe an Olympic athlete trying to win a gold medal. All I know is my chest is seizing and I'm running out of breath.

A quick glance over my shoulder tells me the alpaca is still hot on my heels and not focused on charging our guests.

But what do I do now?

A boat on the lake pulls my attention, reminding me there's a dock here. A dock! Sprinting, I point myself to the long wooden plankway. It feels like it takes hours, yet I'm sure it's only a few seconds until I'm within range. Once there, I fly through the air as I jump from the grassy lawn onto the dock.

My feet slap the planks with a thwack as I barrel down toward the end. I feel something touch my shoulder—a quick look back tells me Chewpaca or Tupaca, or whoever or whatever this animal is called, has caught up to me and I'm out of time.

The end of the dock is closer, the freedom of the lake waiting for me beyond. I get to the end and do the only thing one does when being chased by an out-of-control alpaca toward a lake.

I jump in.

FOURTEEN

Zac

As soon as I realize Etta's jumped in the lake, I charge down the grassy lawn toward the dock. In my rush, I don't notice Brett coming through the trees from the other side, both of us running in a V shape, our connection point being the beginning of the dock.

Out of breath, I stop at the end of the dock as Brett slows down from holding a lead in his hand.

"Stay here, Zac, in case Chewie gets past me." He nods his head at me like we're in this together. "You'll be the last line of defense."

Bracing myself, I say a silent prayer that I won't be steamrolled today by an alpaca, and watch as Brett approaches the out-of-control creature. In the lake just beyond where Brett stands, Etta treads water, keeping an eye on all of us.

Within a few seconds, Brett has the lead back on Chewpaca and is walking him off the dock, both his and the alpaca's head hung low.

"Gosh, I'm so sorry." He looks at me and shakes his head as he indicates to Etta coming out of the water. "Anyone have a towel?"

One of the guys having lunch had been sitting on the ground on a beach towel. He doesn't even think twice before hopping up and racing to Etta's side with it, wrapping it around her.

"Thanks," she manages through chattering teeth before turning to look at Brett. "That was fun."

Lucy, who I'd honestly forgotten about until now, pipes up from a spot she'd commandeered on the ground. Her eyes, full of faux-patheticness, meet mine. "I think I twisted my ankle."

"I can help with that," Brett chimes in beside me. He thrusts the lead in my hand. "Can you hold on to Chewpaca for me while I give this nice young lady an assessment?"

Lucy giggles as Brett kneels beside her, checking her ankle and leg for any signs of an injury. I'm pretty sure she's got another kind of pain going on, one that requires more than a physical checkup. It's also the kind I'm not qualified for, if you catch my drift...so maybe Brett will be.

Turning my attention to Etta, I put an arm around her shivering shoulders in an effort to further warm her up.

"Are you okay?" I say low enough so only she can hear me.

Etta nods. "I'm just cold. You guys go ahead with your bonding activities. I'm going to head to the cabin and take a hot shower."

I keep an eye on her as she meanders over to her cabin and lets herself inside. Shaking my head, I turn my attention back to my team.

Life surely isn't dull when you know Etta McCoy.

The rest of the day ticks along slightly better than the beginning. We conquer our Random Words of Kindness game, and after I catch Lucy laughing about Etta going in the lake, I have everyone make cardboard boats—for our spontaneous boat race for the McCoy Cup, a new event I'm proud of...even if its namesake never rejoins us at the lake for the rest of the afternoon.

When it's time for dinner, Etta shows up. As I walk into the kitchen to start the grill, she's already there making guacamole and salsa.

"I turned the grill on for you about ten minutes ago," she says with a smile as she looks at me, pointing at the bowls in front of her. "Are you ready for some Wholly Frijoles?"

"Is that a Mexican dish?"

"It was the name of a restaurant I loved going to in D.C." She grabs an avocado, scooping it out and plopping its insides into the bowl in front of her, smashing everything together. " 'Loved' being the key word there."

The grill is set up outside the kitchen door, so I step outside and throw a few large pieces of chicken breasts on it before closing it and coming back inside. On the counter is a pile of tortillas.

"Can you get started heating those up?" Etta asks.

"Of course." I turn on the stovetop gas burners and grab her pile of tortillas. "My college roommate showed me this method for heating up tortillas, and it's one I've perfected over the years."

A smile plays on her lips. "Oh really? So you think it's some big secret to warm up your tortillas on a gas burner?"

Tossing one on the burner, I let it flip in the air once before it falls, then shrug. "Can anyone else do dinner and a show like I can?"

"That remains to be seen." Etta chuckles as she grabs a few tomatoes and starts dicing them.

Making sure she's watching me, I do a few more aerial

tricks with my tortillas, including one where I toss it in the air and spin it in place, turning around to catch it and place it on the burner. When I look over, Etta rolls her eyes.

"I hate to be the voice of reason, but I feel like you may get hurt." She's about to say something else when a notification on her cell phone, sitting on the opposite counter, goes off. She walks over and stares at the screen before she closes her eyes and opens her mouth. Wide.

When she stays like that for longer than ten seconds, I tap her shoulder. "You good?"

She opens her eyes. "That was my silent scream. It needed to come out."

"That text is no good?"

"That ex is no good." She pulls her eyes from mine, going back to her chopping duties. "My ex-husband seems to think we have something to talk about. He wants me to make time for him, and that's one thing I don't have much of to give right now. Especially to him."

"Things didn't end well?"

"They ended amicably, at least I thought they did." She shakes her head, holding a knife in the air and waving it as she speaks. As she's slicing the air while her hands are shaky and she seems to be getting worked up, I really hope she doesn't let it go.

I place another tortilla on the burner, and here's where I make my mistake: I chose to look over to see if Etta's okay and not throwing her knife as I do this. However, I don't see the flame as it licks my sleeve, and I don't even realize my arm's on fire until Etta looks up at me, her face shrouded in horror.

By the time I realize what's happening, she's already grabbed a damp dish towel and tosses it over the flame, putting it out.

"Oh my...are you okay?" she asks, her eyes wide.

"I guess I should be glad your brother is in the fire department; it seems the apple doesn't fall far from the tree."

"Not sure if that's the right analogy to use here." She shakes her head, staring at me incredulous.

When we look at my arm, I'm amazed nothing more happened than my sleeve was burned and my hair was singed. "That could have been worse; I shouldn't have been listening to you tell me about your evil ex."

"Don't blame this on me," Etta starts to hiss, but when she looks into my eyes, I know she can tell I'm joking. "I think we need to take a five-minute break."

"Okay." Figuring she probably wants to be alone, I head outside to check the grill. "Where are you going?"

"I'm gonna hang at the grill."

"No, no, just turn the heat down. I want to show you something."

I do as she tells me and follow her out the door. She indicates with her chin across the

parking lot to the two small buildings that sit on the edge, both under renovation. "Follow me."

I trot behind her to the first building. It's in good shape, but when we peek in the windows, I can see it's been ripped apart inside. It's a shell, a hollow vessel in need of more.

"So..." I hold my hands out, unsure why we're here. "Are you going to make me eat my dinner here tonight?"

"This is why I'm so mad at my ex." She presses her nose to the window, peering inside lovingly. "I had what's called an urban winery when I was in D.C. We owned it together, but it was my idea. I found wineries in the area that I worked with, and I brought their wines to my restaurant to show them off. We planned wine tastings, we'd do wine pairing dinners, and held wine parties. You name it...if it could be done with wine, we did it."

"That's a cool idea. I guess it was urban since you were in the city and you didn't have your own vineyard?"

She nods. "Exactly. And, I want to do that right here, in this building. There are so many amazing wineries in the Carolina region, and I want to introduce tourists and our locals to them all."

"You want to replicate what you did in D.C."

"But, I can't." She sighs, stepping away from the window. The sun has gone down, disappearing behind pastel pink and purple lined clouds before we had slipped out of the kitchen, so it's hard for me to see her. The shadows fall across her face, keeping her true feelings hidden from me for the moment. "He's taking me to court over our business, and to top it all off, he's holding a large sum of money, which I'm owed, over my head so I can't use it."

Cue me wanting to give this woman every cent I have in my pocket. "Were you going to use the money to open this place?"

"Basically." Etta steps out of the shadows and back into the parking lot, where lamplight reigns. Her features are dark, and I hear the emotion in her voice as she talks about her old business. "Him taking me to court is hurtful, and he's stopping me from doing what I want, which is to simply start over and just be."

"He won't listen to reason?"

She shakes her head. "He's determined to stop me and I don't know why. I just know he's wasting a lot of people's time with this lawsuit."

"And no one comes out of it feeling good, huh?"

"I guess. I'm not sure why he's decided to pursue this." She shrugs. "People never cease to amaze me."

An alarm on her phone goes off, and Etta starts walking away. She turns around, waving her hand for me to follow her. "Come on. It's time to flip the chicken."

I watch as she trots ahead of me, back to the kitchen. This conundrum of a woman is opening up to me, a tiny crack at a time, and it's nothing short of amazing.

And I'm realizing I would follow her anywhere.

FIFTEEN

Etta

Dinner was delightfully smooth, even with Lucy making sure she squeezed in so she could sit just-thistightandnextto Zac.

For real.

Honestly, it was like watching someone try to stuff a sausage. Zac was sitting next to one of his colleagues, and Lucy had literally pushed the two of them apart and wrenched her way in there.

After excusing myself, I tended to the firepit, getting it going so we could do s'mores as requested and then go to bed. Standing here now, I'm pretty impressed with myself: the fire is raging in a good way, and I've set up the picnic table nearby with all of the s'mores goodies one could want.

"Ohhhh, a fire!" Lucy squeals as she walks out of the kitchen door, wrapping a jacket around her. "Do we have s'mores, too?"

Lucy's voice is beginning to sound like chalk screeching across a chalkboard in my mind. Gritting my teeth, I try to smile. This day needs to be over.

"There's a pile of food on that table over there." Zac appears beside me, pointing to the picnic table.

Lucy slithers to the table, clicking her tongue as she looks at the selection. She spins around and looks my way with narrowed eyes. "No gluten-free graham crackers nor any dark chocolate?"

Mitch the grocer's words reverberate in my ears. "Ohh, I'm sorry, we weren't able to get gluten-free graham crackers."

"Nor any dark chocolate?" Lucy's got a hand on her hip now, and she's looking annoyed. Someone give this woman some sugar, and fast, please.

I shake my head, tossing a quick glance Zac's way, hoping he sees my plea for help.

"Sorry, Lucy, but I see cheesecake bites over there and those are gluten free for sure." Zac points to the table again as he stokes the fire. "It's not a big deal, right?"

Lucy bats her eyelashes and winks at Zac. I'm not sure if she's simply shameless or if it's an act. She walks over and stands beside him, laying her head on his shoulder. "It's no big deal, Zac. I've brought some snacks with me, which I'll whip out when we go to bed tonight."

Somewhere in the pit of my stomach, a bomb goes off. I had forgotten that Lucy and Zac were sharing a cabin together. Granted, there's a few other people in there, but still.

Also, why am I worried about where Zac sleeps anyway?

"So how are things going, team?"

Spinning around, we're all surprised to see Sergeant Lane walking our way.

"Hey, man," Zac says as he steps forward, holding his hand out to shake Lane's. "Didn't think you'd be here until tomorrow."

"I was over helping Brett with his fence." Lane looks my way and winks. "So I thought I'd cut through the woods and surprise you guys." He holds up a gym bag. "Got room for one more?"

I look around and spot my clipboard with the sleeping arrangements on it sitting on the table. I walk toward it, but Zac beats me to it. He's got the file folder open and is flipping through the pages, scanning names.

He looks at Lane. "It's a pretty tight squeeze. Amelia closed the bunk house and we're all sharing the cabins."

Lane peers over his shoulder and indicates a spot on a piece of paper. "I can stay in that cabin with you, Wright. I'll just stay on the floor. No big deal."

"Oh, boy, this is going to be a fun sleepover," Lucy purrs. I've never seen a cat in heat until this very moment, and kids... it ain't pretty.

"No way my superior is going to sleep on the floor." Zac slams the folder shut. "You can have my bed."

"Really? Thanks, Zac. You don't have to do that." He indicates with his head to the folder in Zac's hand. "Will you have a place to sleep?"

"I do." Using the folder, Zac points to the picnic table. "Now, go get some dessert and settle in. Good to have you."

As Lane walks away, Zac sidles up next to me. "So, the cabin you're staying in has an extra bed...right?"

Cold water blasts through my veins. "Say what?"

Zac's eyes are pleading. "Can I stay in your cabin tonight?"

"Here." I toss a pillow at Zac's head, giggling as I do. "Just don't snore, and please don't sleepwalk."

"Someone dealing with some PTSD around snoring and sleepwalking?" Zac asks, a ghost of a smile playing on his lips.

"No, just covering my bases." I leave him alone in the spare bedroom and head back to the master, where I close the door and take my time getting into my pajamas. I start to open the door only to stop myself.

I take a step back and find myself staring at my reflection in the mirror. My hair is a mess, my shirt is on inside out, and my mascara has started to flake off.

"Wow." I say this out loud and to no one in particular. I look like I've given up. Laughing to myself as I straighten my hair, I guess in some ways I almost had. But, things have changed.

Swiping a washcloth from the dresser, I step in the en suite to run some hot water. As I soak the washcloth under the faucet and begin wiping the day off my face, my thoughts start to wander.

Right to Zac.

Sighing, I'm still shocked at my reaction to Lucy. I've been shocked at my reaction to a lot of things lately; I guess Lucy should be no surprise. As I wipe the last of the makeup off and run the cloth under my neck and over my jawline, I find my eyes in the mirror and I smile.

"Now, there's someone I've not seen in a long time." Stepping back, my inclination is to throw moisturizer on and head out the door, but I really look at myself. I've been so mad about Steve and the lawsuit, and angry that he's been holding on to my money, I've felt like I'm being held hostage and have no control...and then there's Zac.

He makes me smile. And I can't deny he's funny and smart. Even though he arrested me, I know he was doing his job. As mad as I was, I was impressed when he didn't let Brett know I was sitting in the cell. If Brett had known, then my brother would have known. Then it would have been all kinds of hairy.

I untuck my top and give myself one last look of approval, happy to see this woman standing in front of me with a huge grin on her face. She looks happy. And I like her. A lot.

I'm still smiling when I make my way out into the shared living area and sit down, putting my feet up on an old steamer trunk that's acting as our coffee table.

"Don't you look like the cat who ate the canary?" Zac says as he lords over me holding two mugs in his hand. "Here, I hope you like hot chocolate."

"Love it." I take the mug from his hands and take a sip. "Perfection. Did you bring hot chocolate with you?"

Zac shrugs, blushing. "Yes, I am a man who loves his hot chocolate and a good quilting session. Now, find me a rerun of *The Golden Girls* and we'll be in business for the night."

I throw my head back and laugh. I even let myself hold on to the laughter for an extra second because it feels so good.

"I've always been a fan of Blanche." I hold my mug high. "She was a cougar before cougars became a thing."

"Why, Etta McCoy," Zac says with a faux Southern drawl as he sits down beside me. "Are you a cougar?"

"No! I mean, n-n-not that I know of?" It's comical that I find myself stuttering right now. Giggling, I turn and angle my body so I'm facing Zac. "If I had been, I wouldn't know it."

"But would you be one...if the relationship calls for it, that is?"

"What kind of inquisition is this?" I manage with a half laugh. "Do we need to throw our drivers licenses down on the table? For the record, I'm thirty."

"Flirty and thirty." Zac whistles. "Well, if we ever date, you would be the cougar."

I sit up and place my mug on the trunk, slapping my palms to my cheeks in surprise. "What?"

"Yes, ma'am. I won't be thirty until December, so you are older than me." Zac leans across me to put his mug on the trunk as well.

"Age is more than a number." I lean closer to him, whispering now. "Cause we both know I'm way more mature than you are."

Zac also leans close, pressing his lips to my ear. "Nuh-uh."

Laughing, I go to lean back, but his hands catch me and pull me back up. In a second, his fingertips are prodding at my side, poking into my middle and around my ribcage, and causing me to laugh in a fit.

"Please! Zac, stop," I'm begging him in between gasps of air and laughter. My hands find his, and I try clenching his digits to pull them away, but he's too strong. He flips me around so I'm on my back on the couch and then stands over me, letting his fingers continue their walk.

"Come on, Etta." His nose touches mine. "Admit it. I'm mature, too. Come on."

"I can't admit anything unless you stop," I manage, relieved when his fingers come to an unmoving halt. But they stay planted where they land, as if he's ready to start up again.

"Okay, I stopped. Unless you admit I'm also mature"—he wiggles his digits, causing me to squirm—"it's more tickle. So?"

Opening my mouth, I slam my eyes into his, ready with a retort on the tip of my tongue. It was a comeback to rule all comebacks, but something in his look stops me. His eyes follow mine, and I taste his breath as it hits my lips. My hands fly to his face, stroking his jawline as he drags a finger up to my cheek.

Zac drops his head so the tip of his nose caresses my neck and the heat of his breath ripples across my skin. Sighing, I let out a gasp of air as I let my fingers thread their way through his tresses and pulled him closer to me.

His hands are firm and strong, his grip cinching around my waist as he pulls me up with him, holding me and looking at me as we sit tangled on the tiny couch in the small living room of the cabin. The smell of cedar surrounds us, but so does sandalwood and clean sheets, Zac's signature scent.

My hands dance along his arms, which wrap around my middle as he clutches me and pulls me close, his lips dropping and slanting across mine. I let my body respond in kind and pull his head closer, allowing me to press my lips firmer onto his. And I'm not stopping him because I don't want him to stop.

This kiss isn't like any other kiss I've had before. Not one with Steve and not from anyone I've dated ever. This kiss with Zac is what I would imagine happens when explosives and firecrackers get married. It's hot and it crackles with heat and energy, and I am seeing stars.

But...there's always a but, isn't there? Dropping my hands to my sides, I pull away, taking a moment to catch my breath. When I look Zac's way, I see he's doing the same but also keeping one eye on me.

A tiny smile dances on the ends of his lips as he reaches out a hand to push a few strands of hair away from my eyes.

"Hi." His whisper is throaty, sexy.

"Hey," I croak before cackling. "Sorry." I clear my throat and Zac laughs.

"Yeah, I didn't expect that, either." He chews on his bottom lip as he watches me. I'm still over here trying to calm my heart rate down.

When I allow my eyes to find his, I know that in a second we could start this whole thing all over again—but we can't. And not because I'm the cougar, but because I'm going to lay down the law. For now.

"I really don't know where to go from here." I'm half joking, half not. So I do what my defense mechanism tells me to do: I start to retreat.

Glancing at my watch, I tap its face. "I'm wiped, and we need to get up early."

"Me, too," Zac says, standing. He holds his hand out, and I place mine inside his, letting him help me to my feet. We stand close, looking at one another for what seems like ages before I pull away.

"I'm gonna go…" I point to the master bedroom door. "Alone, that is. To my room."

"That's fine with me." Zac's eyes are laughing now even if his mouth isn't. "I'm gonna go to that room now," he says as he points to his door. "Alone. By myself. If I hear any cougars scratching at my door to get in, I'll call the local vet. You hear me?"

Is it awkward? I guess. Weird? For sure. Am I wondering how we're going to handle this? You bet I am.

But first I need to get in my room. I grip the door handle and swing the door open, turning around to look at Zac one more time before I close it.

"Do you wanna talk about what just happened, McCoy?" Zac asks me, his head tilted to the side.

"Later," I whisper. "It's late."

"Okay." Zac throws one last sultry grin my way. "Night, Etta."

"Night, Zac."

Ever so softly, I close the door behind me. As it closes, I lean my back against it and slowly slide to the floor with my fingertips touching the spot on my mouth where Zac's lips were holding court just a mere few minutes ago.

What is this man doing to me?

SIXTEEN

Etta

When I stand here and look outside, I have the perfect view of the lake whose tranquil waters glint seafoam green today, the woods which surround us, and of Zac and his team of stoic police officers (and Lucy)...bonding over an egg relay race.

Even though the last twenty-four hours have been pretty tough, I have a feeling of satisfaction inside as I clean up and put everything away. Glancing at my watch, I know they'll be gone in a few hours and then I can go home and sleep in my bed. I've worked one event for Amelia and I'm already worn out.

And then there's Zac. My fingertips fly to my lips, thinking about his kiss last night. His lips were so soft, and when I close my eyes, I swear I can still feel their soft heat on mine. I softly groan, closing my eyes and letting myself float back to that moment.

Opening my eyes again, I shake it off and go back to wiping down the counters. I've been such a porcupine lately, I'm honestly in shock that Zac and I even kissed. I mean, he's Zac Wright. He could have anyone, like Lucy. She's annoying, but she's like a police version of Barbie. Yes, she annoys me, but I can admit it's because she was flirting with Zac.

Which brings me back to my feelings for him...where has all of this come from?

I'm still working out the semantics when I notice a car making its way up the long driveway from the main road to the campground. It's a weekday, so it could be someone coming to see Amelia, but she would have warned me if there was a meeting. It won't be a camper because we put up a sign saying there isn't any space.

Throwing a tea towel over my shoulder, I head outside to greet the visitor. I watch as the white Chevrolet enters the parking lot, clearly a rental. I wave, trying to provide a beacon for what I'm determining must be a weary traveler in need of some advice.

But when the car rolls to a stop and I see who's behind the steering wheel, I'm ready to douse my light with water and tell this guy to take a long walk off a short dock.

Spinning on my heel, I hear the car door open and shut and the sound of his feet crunching on the gravel as he jogs to my side.

"Etta, don't walk away. I told you I wanted to talk."

I feel a vise-like grip on my forearm, forcing me to whip around. Glaring at the hand, I drag my eyes up to meet his. "Steve, you need to let go of me—now. See all of those people having fun down by the lake? They're the local police."

Steve drops his hand from my arm like it's a hot potato. I know he's not here to hurt me—he's not the type—but sometimes you need to be strong with people like him. People that don't take no for an answer.

"Etta, I want us to fix this. I'm here to fix us."

"There's no us to fix, we're divorced. But there's the fact you're suing me. I guess if you want to fix that you need to... oh, I don't know. Drop the lawsuit?"

"Etta, the idea for the business was ours. We started it together, we grew it together."

"No, we didn't, Steve. Your amnesia is perfectly timed when it comes to the facts, isn't it?"

"I'm not trying to take it from you, I just think we're better served if I make it into a chain."

I shake my head. "I don't want to talk about this right now. You kind of ruined things the minute you had me served. Have your lawyer call mine, and we'll go from there."

Backing away, I start to head inside, but Steve appears in front of me, holding his hands out to stop me. "Come on. Can we have a coffee at least. For old times' sake?"

I start to shake my head, but when I do, Steve's arms open wide and he closes in for an embrace. I feel my shoulders hike up to my ears as his arms wrap around my body, my hands at my sides.

So awkward.

We're not here long before I hear someone clear their throat. Grateful for the reprieve, I jumped away from Steve, surprised to find Zac standing in front of us.

"I was looking for you." Zac's eyes bounce from me to Steve and back again. "All good?"

"We're fine," Steve interrupts, stepping forward and holding his hand out to shake Zac's. "Steve Shaw, Etta's ex-husband."

Zac's gaze slides to mine, and he winks. Suddenly, I feel a warmth as his hand wraps around mine. He holds out his other hand to shake Steve's. "I'm Zac. And I'm not Etta's ex anything."

Steve's face glows various shades of red as I bite my lip, trying not to let the laughter escape that's building inside.

"I'd like to say it's a pleasure, but..." Steve looks at Zac's hand, but ignores it. His eyes flash with irritation as they rock between me and Zac, with a pit stop of him staring at my hand in Zac's.

"Etta, what's it going to take for me to get time alone with you?" Steve's tone is clipped, his jaw tense.

"It's going to take a lot more than you showing up while I work." I feel a bit of my own irritation surge forward. "How did you know where I was, Steve?"

"You mentioned it," he lies.

I fight the urge to yell, instead choosing to be civil. "I wouldn't have told you about this place; I don't normally work here. I'm doing this"—I wave my arms around, indicating the campground and its surroundings—"as a favor. So, back to my question. How?"

Steve shifts his weight from one foot to the other, refusing to make eye contact with me. I let go of Zac's hand and put both of mine on my hips. This is starting to stink.

"Steve Shaw, you need to tell me how you found me."

I can tell he's embarrassed. We were married, and I remember his tells. No eye contact means he's done something he never should have in the first place.

He eyes Zac and shoves his hands in his front jean pockets. Steve's Adam's apple bobs up and down as he swallows. "I used the 'find my phone' app."

Of course. Dropping my hands from my hips, I throw them in the air instead. "You tracked me?"

"I did what I needed to do." Steve's tone is defensive and his eyes are wide. "Was it a bad thing?"

"It's not the nicest thing you can do. We're no longer together, so technically you don't need to have that app connected to my phone anymore, do you?" I hold my hand out. "Give me your phone, Steve."

Beside me, Zac's shoulders rise and fall from silent laughter while Steve's takes on the rounded shape of insecurity. Slowly, he places his phone in the palm of my hand.

I tap the last code that I remember him having and it still works. In a matter of seconds, I delete the app and give his phone back to him. I know this app, and luckily when you delete it, all the information is erased so there's no way he can track me again.

"Sorry," he says, defeated. With a scowl he opens the driver's side door, stopping before he climbs behind the wheel. "I'm staying in town at the Harper B&B. I'm here through the weekend. I really hope you'll find time to talk to me."

Steve shuts the door and reverses out of his parking space. I stay standing stock-still in my spot until I see his car disappear down the driveway. I need to know he's gone so I can relax.

Beside me, Zac lets out a huge breath of air. "I'm sorry for that. Instinct kicked in when I saw him, and it took over when he said his name was Steve."

"Not at all, thank you." Wrapping my arms around my middle, I hug myself. "At least, for the moment, he thinks I'm dating someone. Maybe he won't be as pushy next time I see him or at least not try to force his way into a conversation with me."

"He seems desperate," Zac murmurs, standing closer to me. He raises a hand, brushing away some stray strands of hair from my face. "Like he's only now realizing what he lost."

Is his touch like a spark of fire? Completely. Feeling exposed, my eyes dart around to see if anyone is watching us. I'm not surprised to find Lucy glowering at me from across the lawn. If she could throw a dagger at my heart right now, I know she'd do it.

Zac's fingertips brush my forehead again, and my eyes flick back to meet his. A familiar flutter takes over inside my chest as a warm heat rises to my cheeks. "Please..."

"I can tell you this much," Zac whispers, his lips pressed against my ear. "If I had you, I would never let you go."

"...stop." My everything tingles. The overwhelm is too much, so I take a step back to get some air. "What are we doing, Zac?"

"Flirting?" Zac cocks his head to one side, grinning.

Oh, that smile of his. It's like a sucker punch to the side of my head. "Well, you're not wrong."

"Let's fix this, shall we?" Laughing, Zac takes a step closer to me and takes my hand. "How about you and I go on a date?"

"Us?" Pulling my hand away, I point to myself and crane my neck to see if someone is standing nearby filming this. Is he being serious? "On a date?"

Zac nods his head, keeping those green eyes trained on me. "Yep."

"A date where you pick me up and we go to dinner and maybe a movie?" This is getting interesting. Still confusing, but interesting, too.

"Kind of. More like, I'll pick you up and we'll go to the charity fundraiser together next weekend." He looks at me and smiles, showing off the most perfect set of teeth I've ever seen. "What do you say—will you do me the honor?"

There's no excuse to say no, and I have no wall up. It's like my tractor beam stopped working and I can finally let my guard down. "Okay."

"Okay." He nods his head back toward the lakefront. "I need to get back to those folks and finish up so we can all get out of here, but we'll talk later. Settle the finer details."

I watch him walk away from me and marvel at how long I can tread water this confusing.

I'm going on a date. A date with Zac Wright.

I just hope Mr. Wright doesn't end up being Mr. Wrong.

SEVENTEEN

Zac

There's one place close to town where I know I can go anytime for someone to hang out with. My grandparents would say I'm craving fellowship, my parents would say it's my longing for community, but for me...I just need some other guys I can talk to and not feel so alone trying to navigate things like...Etta.

Walking up the sidewalk to Dubs's Garage, I already feel like any stress I have is easing from my neck and shoulders. Dubs's Garage is owned by the one and only Dubs Williams, a part-timer at the Lake Lorelei Fire Department. His garage is the place to go if you need work done to your car, and he has special deals for public servants. I'd dropped my cruiser off here for an oil change yesterday.

Seeing as he's just that kind of cool, he's also managed to create a spot for hanging out. Where the men who live in the area like to congregate. We're talking pool tables, pinball machines, Pacman, Ms. Pacman...and I think he added Frogger to his collection recently. It's gamer heaven.

"I was wondering if you'd get here on time," Dubs calls

out when he sees me, grabbing an old cloth to wipe the grease off his hands.

"On time?" Glancing at my watch, I see there's fifteen minutes until the shop closes. "You doubted I'd be here before you closed?"

"Actually," Dubs says with a chuckle as he indicates with his thumb toward the door leading to the back room, "those guys in there are worried."

Opening the door, I'm surprised-ish to see Brett sitting across the table from Sergeant Lane, throwing down cards on the table in front of him.

"There he is," Lane calls out. "Got a beer over here with your name on it and a seat if you want to buy in and play a round."

"Poker?" I ask, taking the beer from Brett's outstretched hand.

Lane grins. "What else?"

Turning around, I find the old guy standing with his arms crossed, watching me with a bit of a twinkle in his eye. Dubs shrugs his shoulders.

"I've been meaning to have some guys over for a card game and figured today was as good as any."

"I'd have to agree with you, Dubs." Taking a sip of my beer, my phone chimes in my pocket. Sliding it out, I peek at the screen to see Tuck's texting me. Turning to the room, I hold my phone in the air.

"Do you guys mind if I invite one more person? My brother's in town again."

There's a general wave of hands and a grunt from Dubs, giving me all the permission I need. I flick Tuck the address, then pull up a chair beside Dubs.

"How's life going for you, Zac?" The old man's eyes are gentle. "You like it here?"

"Sweetkiss is great." Technically, Dubs's Garage is in Lake Lorelei, which is the town over from Sweetkiss Creek, but the two towns and one other, Taylortown, all make up an area known as Love Valley. "I can't complain at all. I like my job..."

"You're just saying that cause I'm sitting right here," Lane murmurs, his eyes on his cards.

Dubs points to Brett. "Did this one tell you his news?"

"He did. Congrats again, Brett. Be good to have you in town." I clink his beer bottle with mine and toast the news. "How's Chewpaca doing?"

"Chewie and Tupaca are settling in just fine, now that I have a fully fenced-in section on my lot for them." Brett rolls his eyes as Lane puts his cards down on the table, jumping up as he does with his hands in the air.

"Royal flush, baby!!" Pumping a fist in the air, Lane sings a refrain from Queen's "We are the champions" as he marches in a parade of one around the room.

"Winner buys dinner," Dubs proclaims, his phone going off in his hand. He glances at it before turning it my way so I can see. "I installed cameras the other day, so now I can see who's coming in the garage no matter where I am."

On the screen is Tuck, making his way through the garage, his neck craning as he looks for me. We watch as he spots the door to the back room and makes his way over and knocks before trepidatiously opening it, ever so slowly.

"Hello?"

Brett, who is already up on his feet, flings the door open, scaring Tuck out of his skin. Once the panic washes away from Tuck's face, the two men shake hands, Brett making sure Tuck has a libation as well before he and Lane turn to the dartboard.

Tuck nods his head in the direction of the dartboard. "We gonna play a game later?"

"Calm down," I mutter, laughing. "I'm worn out from

the retreat. I don't know if I have any competitive edge in my system."

Tuck laughs. "You're gonna need all the competitive edge you can get now that you've taken my bet."

"What bet?" Dubs asks.

Tuck takes a swig of his beer before speaking. "I bet Zac he couldn't seal the deal with a certain wild child who doesn't seem to have a good taste in her mouth when it comes to my brother."

"Actually..." I hold a finger up, wanting to prove him wrong. "We made progress this week. We were stuck at adult camp together overnight and I made the most of it."

Did that last part come out of my mouth sounding a little gross? If I had to judge it off the look Dubs gives me, it's more than gross.

"You'd best be careful." Dubs's Southern drawl is more pronounced than usual. "She's one special lady, and if you break her heart, you're gonna have a few people to answer to, you got that?"

Holding up my hands in surrender, I shake my head apologetically. "Hey, I do not plan on breaking anyone's heart."

"You just want to win the baseball card, right?"

As Tuck says the words, Dubs's right eye twitches. "You made a bet, using Etta, for a baseball card?"

Yeah. It sounds bad. Real bad. I hold my hands out to my sides. "Kind of?"

The disappointment reflected in Dubs's expression pierces my heart. "You'd better tell me it's not about just a card."

"It really isn't. I mean, with him"—I nod my head toward my brother—"it is, because I want that card from him."

Dubs crosses his arms in front of him. "How does that make it any better?"

"Well, for me," I say, my voice a little lower, "I guess it's motivation so I step up."

Dubs tilts his head to one side. "Step up?"

"To ask her out. In a weird way it gave me more confidence to ask her on a date."

Dubs looks at me thoughtfully. "Etta's been scary lately, it's okay. You can say it."

I shrug. "I get the feeling she's not usually like this. In fact, she's mentioned it, too."

"I like that woman. She's put a lot on the line to move down here to be with her family. The Etta I met through her brother is kind, giving, has an open heart, and would give you the last dollar in her wallet if you needed it." Dubs shakes his head. "Ever since that lawsuit landed on her front step, she's been a bit more irritable than usual."

I nod in agreement. "I met her ex."

"And?"

"Not impressed."

"Good." Dubs sits closer to me, tossing an arm around my shoulders as someone else's phone goes off in the room. "Glad we understand each other."

"You've got to be kidding me!"

Snapping my head to see what the commotion is, I find Lane staring at the phone in his hands, shaking his head. He looks up, his eyes finding mine, and motions for me to come over. I'm across the room and by his side in a few strides, peering over his shoulder at the screen.

It's an email from the state. The kind of email that is akin to a "Dear John" letter. A government "it's not you, it's us" excuse.

"What's up?" Dubs asks, flanked by an equally confused Tuck and Brett.

"The grant we applied for, for the canine therapy unit."

Lane shakes his head and shoves his phone back in his pocket. "We didn't get it."

Am I bummed? Yes. I'd spent a lot of time working on the grant and had my hopes up that we'd get it.

"So, what happens now?" Tuck questions.

"It's not the end of the world; we're still fundraising and we even have the charity ball next week, but it means we can't start as soon as we hoped." Shrugging my shoulders, I grab a barstool and sit down. "We'll get there, it's just going to take a lot longer."

Lane sighs. "Time is one of those things that isn't on our side with this. The sooner we have a unit like this in motion, the better it is for our community and for our policing."

He looks my way and holds his bottle in the air. "Here's to you, Zac. You did a lot to try to get it over the line. We'll try again next year."

As Tuck and Brett start throwing darts and warming up for a game, Lane marches up to my side. "So, did I overhear you say you made a bet with Etta as the prize?"

I'm beginning to understand how small-town rumors get started now.

Tuck pipes up as he tosses his first dart. "No, it's a bet with a baseball card as the prize."

"Oh?" His eyes wide, Brett chuckles as he shakes his head. "You'd better tell her about this."

"Why?"

"Do you like her?" Brett asks.

My eyes bounce back and forth from Dubs, to Tuck, to Lane, then back to Brett, who still shakes his head from side to side. I'm man enough to admit it.

"I do."

"Then tell her." Dubs pats me on the back as he walks past. "So she knows ahead of time. It won't matter if you do like her and have wanted to date her forever—if she finds out after the fact, she'll ghost you."

Tuck's about to toss a second dart when he stops himself. "You really think you may like her? Like, like her, like her?"

Rolling my eyes, I bump a shrug. "What are we, stuck in middle school for life? Yes, I like her, like her. But..."

"But what?" Tuck repeats.

"But it's a small town. But I know what she's going through. But I make her crazy. But the timing isn't right..."

"I love a good excuse, don't you, Brett?" Lane asks, winking.

"The only excuse I want to hear is when someone explains to me why we're not finishing up this game right now." Brett holds his darts up and tips his chin at the board. "Tuck, step aside."

"And we thought we were competitive," Tuck whispers in a hushed tone as the other two get back to their game.

"Yeah, I think my knack for getting fired up and wanting to win could have gotten me into trouble this time." I grab a seat at the small kitchen table and park it. "I need to tell her about us making this bet so she doesn't think the only reason I wanted to ask her out was to win."

Tuck makes a face. "Wasn't it?"

I smack Tuck's arm. "Not the point. The winning got me spurred on, but if we're honest, I took the bet for Etta. Don't forget, twice you tried to get me to take the bet and I said no."

"True," Tuck concurs. "So...what now?"

"I do what I need to do. I'll talk to her before the fundraiser and set everything straight."

"You do realize if she pulls out of going, technically you won't win the bet."

I'm starting to understand why sibling rivalry is a thing. "Tuck, I don't care."

But I do care about what Etta thinks. Pulling my phone out of my pocket, I find her name and send her a quick text before crossing my fingers.

I need her to hear this from me so she doesn't get the wrong idea.

EIGHTEEN

Etta

Having time to weed my long neglected gardens is absolute joy for me. I love autumn days. It's still warm but cool enough for a long-sleeved shirt. The sun isn't beating down, so extended time outside doesn't cause me any kind of heat stroke while I'm exerting my energy.

Sitting on my front steps sipping a glass filled with ice cold lemonade, I watch Thor and Herc as they roll around in the freshly mowed grass. Coming back home from the retreat with a to-do list a mile long, I'd woken up this morning ready to attack it, but oddly found myself losing energy and motivation as the day progressed.

Since moving here, life has been like a small car stuffed with clowns. I know the car is there, and I know the clowns are in it, but I don't know what clown is gonna come out first...and let's make one thing very clear: I don't like clowns.

Moving to Sweetkiss Creek was supposed to be my new chapter, starting over. I closed the door and thought we were moving on, but with the stink that is Steve still pungent in the air, it turns out I shoulda nailed that sucker shut.

Steve. I'll never understand how we got here. We'd been

together for about three years and I think he thought asking me to marry him was what he was supposed to do—like me saying yes was what I thought I was supposed to do.

I'd realized a couple years in that we'd already grown apart. When the time came to discuss it, I had worried for weeks about talking to him about my feelings. In the end, I didn't need to; he had listened with open ears and we'd agreed mutually that we're better friends and business partners.

I almost choke on an ice cube when I think that last part. Business partners. My former business partner is now trying to sue me and accomplish what...tying my hands? The pit in my stomach sloshes around, feeling like an acid storm or some kind of explosion. If only I could impress on Steve the stress he's causing, but I'd rather have my fingernails pulled out one at a time, thank you very much.

I tip the glass back and drink the last drop of my lemonade as a car slows down and turns into my driveway. Both dogs freeze in their spots, watching as the vehicle rolls slowly toward the house. It's not a car I recognize, but the driver is.

As the driver's side door opens, I set my glass down and stand up, putting my hands on my hips and watching the dogs race over and bark at the car's occupant. "You don't take no for an answer well, do you?"

Shielding his eyes from the sun rays dipping behind my house, Steve cocks his head to one side. "I figured if I came to you, I may get further than trying to text you, or call, or email..."

"Or go through lawyers?"

She shoots, she scores, folks. I watch as his head dips. Are his cheeks red with embarrassment, or did he have the heat up in his car?

"That is fair." Steve holds his hands in front of him in surrender while Thor and Hercules circle him happily. "I come in peace. Are you alone, or is your boyfriend here?"

"I'm alone." I thread my arms across my chest stubbornly. "What do you want?"

He walks forward and points to the chairs on my porch. "Can we sit and talk at least?"

Watching the dogs sniff his ankles, a part of me wishes one of them would bite him. But they're my dogs and I trained them well. And Steve was always good to them, so of course they're excited to see him. Still, it's a lot to handle, so I open the front door and shoo them inside before I take a seat, indicating to Steve to take the other.

"Okay," I say, sitting back and crossing one leg over the other. "Talk."

"I want to talk about the lawsuit."

"You know you don't have any right to that lawsuit, don't you?"

"I wanted to get your attention."

"Oh you have it, alright. You got my attention. Now, what do you want?"

Steve clasps his hands. "I never wanted it to get this far. My lawyer is furious with me. The judge called him and told him our case would be chucked out and that I was gonna lose."

"Because it's frivolous."

"I know, and I don't need to be reminded." The expression that flashes across his face tells me he's sorry before he even says it. "Sorry, I'm just mad at myself."

"Why are you doing any of this?" Shaking my head, I stand up and walk across to the other side of the porch from where he sits. I work hard to control my voice as I speak. "We had an agreement. Things were fine when we split up and decided to go our separate ways. You never said a thing about wanting the business for yourself or making it a chain or whatever it is you wanted to do at the time we were getting a divorce. Why now?"

"I didn't know at that time that you were leaving, as in moving," Steve blurts out in a rush, his words toppling over one another.

"Why does it matter?"

"Because you were also leaving me."

I'd been leaning against the porch rail, but now I stand up straight. "But we're not together anymore, Steve. It shouldn't matter."

"But it did. It does. To me." He stands up, pacing the porch. "I had nothing before we met, and you had your winery. You were so happy with it; it was your dream and your passion. Man, I was thrilled when I got to be a part of the business with you. However, it was clear the whole time I was there that it was yours. All yours. The employees only really wanted to listen to you. You knew the wines, you had the relationships with your vendors…"

"You could have that as well, and you should since you bought me out." I wag a finger at him. "Which you still owe me the payment for, lest I remind you that it's being held hostage for some strange reason?"

"Don't you see, I wanted something of *my* own."

"I get that, but did you think the best way to find your own dream was to try to stop me from seeing mine through?" I reach out and grab Steve's shoulders, stopping him in front of me so I can look into his eyes. I need him to see my sincerity and the hurt. "You're hurting me. I don't have any way to open my business here yet. You've sued me, so I had to retain a lawyer with money I don't have."

But there's a darkness in his eyes milling about. I drop my hands and step away, leaning against the railing again as he pulls his car keys out of his pocket and jogs to the car. Steve opens the door and reaches in, grabbing a folder, then he runs back up to the porch with it.

"Here." He shoves the folder in my hands.

I hold it up without looking inside. "What is it?"

"Well," he says with a sigh, "it's a document for you to sign. A non-compete clause."

"What?" Now this man has officially gone crazy. I open the folder to make sure he's not joking, and surprise of all surprises, right there in black and white is a piece of paper labeled with the words "non-compete" at the top.

"You're joking." I slam the folder closed and then slam it against his chest. "You're in D.C. and I'm in North Carolina. There's no competition."

"But there could be." Placing the folder on the seat cushion, Steve shoves his hands in his front pockets and won't look at me. "Someone offered me the opportunity to franchise the idea, make the urban winery into a chain."

As the dots start to connect, I feel my blood pressure rise. "You wanted to have the rights to the restaurant so you could sell it and make money off a franchise, is that right?"

As he tries to explain, I laugh a little demented giggle and point to his car. "You should go. Now."

"Etta, I need you to listen to me first…"

I shake my head and wag a finger in the air as I step back inside my front doorway. "We're done."

And I close the door.

Lying in bed, I grab the remote and look for a television station I can stomach. When I can't find anything, I'm happy to turn it off and stare at the ceiling. I've got two dogs in bed with me who need my attention and pets, anyway.

Steve's visit had been an unwelcome blip in my day. I never got a chance to finish the garden, but I did come inside and make a start getting one of the guest bedrooms ready for painting, which was next on my list. A never-ending list to keep me busy until...

Until what? Until Steve finally releases my funds? Until I'm able to use that money to open my wine shop?

I'm good at going down a rabbit hole, but thankfully my phone dings signaling a text and it brings me out of my spiral. Zac's text asking me to meet for a coffee tomorrow morning is a welcome reprieve for me.

My new faux boyfriend. The man who put me in jail. The olive oil to my water...they say opposites attract, but I never believed them. Whoever "they" are.

Look at me now, wishing I could say yes to coffee—with the man I swore I'd never share my air with—but having to text a "no, thank you, wish I could" because I already have plans. Staring at my phone won't make me say yes, and it sure won't change my plans, but I can see the little bubble appear telling me he's replying, so I wait.

For the second time today, I catch myself. *I'm* waiting for him to reply? Shaking my head, I can only grin stupidly. A big, stupid, silly one, the kind I've not enjoyed since...huh. Since I don't know when. I mean, I've smiled since I moved here and had some laughs, but not like this.

This smile is my secret smile, and it's all for me. This smile is one that's excited, because it knows there are more smiles like this one on the horizon. The kind of smile that makes my cheeks hurt and my insides feel giddy and happy and gooey, like they're made up of hot caramel.

It's a smile that's stuck to my face because of one person in particular.

This one's for Zac.

NINETEEN
Zac

"Did you really have your tuxedo dry cleaned and delivered here?"

Lane stands in front of my desk, holding a plastic-covered suit. He balances the hanger on his finger as he swings it in the air.

"It's for the fundraiser next week." Pushing my chair back, I swipe the garment from his hand and cross the room, hanging it on a bolt protruding from the wall. "I was going to pick it up tomorrow, but now my brother is coming through town again with a work buddy and wants to stay the night with me. This was the only way I knew I could do it without forgetting."

"You're fancy. I'm wearing a hand-me-down suit I got from my dad," Lane says, chortling.

"You going to give me grief for owning a tux?"

"Not at all, but"—he inclines his head toward the front lobby—"that's not the only package that arrived for you today."

A little part of me fires up with excitement. I've spent the last few days trying to get Etta alone so we could talk—or rather, so I could explain to her about the bet. Guys making bets and having a woman involved feels pretty archaic, not that she's the prize to be won...which sounds even worse. The last thing I want is for her to think the bet started for some twisted reason to mess with her, and I'm not sure if she's going to understand how it was more about me and Tuck and the baseball card, and less about her.

Nope. Still sounds bad in my mind when I run through it.

In a few quick strides, I'm in the lobby, peering over the counter at one adorable schnauzer, sitting and looking at me with his tongue out and panting away.

"Thor? You're here again?"

At the sound of his name, he's up on his back legs with front paws waving in the air. I make my way around the reception desk and into the lobby to pick him up. The little guy immediately nestles into my arms and snuggles in.

Well, he may not be Etta, but he's a close second. I make my way back to my desk, stopping every few steps for Thor to be pet and rubbed as we go. It's fair to say he's fast becoming a station favorite.

Settling back in at my desk, I make sure Thor's comfy on my lap before shooting a text to Etta, letting her know he's here.

"I think you're fast becoming the local dog whisperer." Lane's appeared back in front of my desk, this time pulling a chair around with him and sitting down across from me.

"I've always had this connection with dogs," I say with a shrug, running my fingers through Thor's fur. "Can't explain it, but my mom has always joked I must have Milk-Bones in my blood."

"I saw on your resume that you were the head trainer for the first canine unit for one of the smaller police stations near Beaufort."

"Up until then, I was volunteering my training skills. I

worked with a group in Georgia to help them get their dogs ready for the blind foundation, then went to Charleston and helped train response dogs for mountain rescue. When my boss asked if I wanted to try my hand at training their first canine unit, you bet I said yes."

"This is why I know you'll be the best person to run our canine therapy team—if we can ever get it off the ground."

"Not getting the grant really hurts, doesn't it?"

Lane nods. "We're just shy of fifteen grand that needs to be raised. Once we have that, we'll be able to break ground and start building the space."

"Everything's approved that needs to be?"

"The local council knows how beneficial this will be not only for the residents, but for the town. Brings in jobs, more people, you know, all positives."

"We have a goal." Crossing my fingers, I hold them up in the air. "If we raise that money, I'd love to put my hat in the ring for the job of running the program."

"No worry there, friend," Lane says, standing up and pushing his chair back to where it was. "You can consider it yours; let's just get those funds raised."

As Lane walks away, my cell phone pings on my desk. Glancing at the screen, I see a text flash from Etta: *I'm outside the station.*

I look down at my furry friend and pat his head.

"Come on, Momma's waiting."

"Thor!" Etta calls out his name and falls to her knees, holding her arms open wide. "Where did you go?"

Thor wriggles himself free of my grasp and hits the ground running, launching himself into her arms.

"I'm not sure why he keeps running away." Etta clips his

leash on his collar and stands, tilting her head to one side and grinning my way.

"Maybe he's trying to get us together, like if this was one of those rom-com movies, he'd be our meet-cute."

"You know what a meet-cute is?"

"I have a sister who made me watch those movies a lot when we were growing up."

"Do you quilt while you watch them?"

"You're funny, aren't you?" Across the street from us the Brickhouse Coffee truck is bustling and the aroma of coffee assaults my senses—and I'm seeing my chance to talk to Etta. "Want a cup of coffee before you go?"

"Sounds good."

We cross the street, with me fighting the urge to wrap an arm around this woman protectively. As we queue in line, my stomach burns with nervousness. This is a conversation I want to get out of the way, and in order to drink my coffee and not throw it up, I think I'm going to need to come clean first.

After we order our drinks, I offer to wait for them while Etta finds a bench nearby for us to sit on. It's not long before I have two large coffees in my hand and I'm sitting beside her under an old magnolia tree.

"So," she begins, "I'm sorry I've been cagey about getting together since the retreat. I had a visitor at my place the other day."

"Oh?"

"My ex."

My fear of telling her about the bet is forgotten, replaced with a worrying tug named Steve. "How was that?"

She lifts a shoulder and lets it drop. "It was intense. I'm so confused as to why he wants things to be so chaotic between us, but I know I can't do anything about it. All I can do is take care of myself and how I feel. I can't control what he does."

Taking a sip of my coffee, I nod my head and listen. As a

man, it's taken me a long time to realize that sometimes someone just wants to talk, and that time might be right now. So I'm gonna listen.

"I keep telling myself this will all be over soon, but if I'm to be honest, I'm scared of what the outcome will be," she continues. "No matter what it is, we're changed forever."

She turns and looks at me. "I'm sorry, I don't need to talk to you about my ex."

"It's okay." I want to tell her I like that she's confiding in me more. That I can feel some of her tension easing away when I'm near. I want to let her know that she can talk to me about whatever she wants; I'm here to be an ear or a shoulder or whatever she needs.

But I can't until I come clean, tell her about that dumb bet I made with Tuck.

Now, serendipitously, I have a chance. I have a chance right now to walk her through the whole thing...and I think she'll hear it and understand why I did it.

Right?

Beside me, Etta plays with Thor's fur as she sips her coffee, her teal-blue eyes flicking to mine. I forgot about those peepers of hers. Like a vacuum, they suck me in and I've already forgotten what I want to say.

"Oh!" With a start, Etta jumps up and looks at her watch. "I need to get going. I forgot I have a mani appointment this afternoon I need to get to, but I need to drop someone off at home first." She points to Thor sitting at her feet. "I don't want to point a paw of blame, but..."

"Oh, yeah, of course." I hop up beside her. There's still a chance for me here and I intend to take it. "But you know, I've been wanting to get some time alone with you."

She turns to me, her face full of concern, and puts a hand on my arm. "Is everything okay?"

I'm opening my mouth when Thor decides to jump up

and launch himself at a passerby eating a hot dog. The next few minutes are a mashup of ketchup and mustard flying, Thor taking off and hiding under the park bench with the hot dog, and Etta shoving a ten-dollar bill in some stranger's hand to pay for the hot dog her dog just ate out of their hand.

This woman. Is. A. Whirlwind.

"Okay, now I'm really late." Etta makes sure the leash is securely clipped on Thor before she takes off, jogging to her car. She turns around and waves to me as she goes. "Talk later?"

I have no choice, do I? I wave and nod, watching her as she reverses out of her parking space and takes off down the street —at a reasonable speed, but takes off nonetheless.

So maybe this time I didn't get the chance to tell her about the bet. But I will. I have to. She can't find out from anyone else.

I guess it's just like Justin Timberlake said.

It's gonna be me.

TWENTY

Etta

I'm still behind the steering wheel when my phone chimes on the seat beside me. Making sure the gear is in park, I grab it and grin. At this point, I would have thought I'd be used to having Zac text me, but it's still new. It was only a mere two weeks ago I was comparing him to sandpaper.

My well-manicured fingers dance across my screen, tapping it to read the message.

ZAC: *Are you free for breakfast? There's something I want to talk to you about.*

Normally, I'd see a text like this from someone, especially a guy, and my heart would immediately pack up and shut down. My stomach would turn and flip, then tie itself in a knot while I try to think through all of the possible horrible things that I could be about to find out.

This is different, though. I think Zac and I are way past that.

ME: *Can't today. At campground with girls. Want to do a late lunch or early dinner?*

ZAC: *I work tonight. Take three: how about a drink tomorrow night?*

I stare out the windshield with a lopsided, goofy smile making its way effortlessly across my face. Yesterday's coffee, he's after a date for breakfast...which is now drinks tomorrow night. Whatever it is he has to tell me must be good if it can't wait until our date night at the fundraiser.

ME: *Perfect. Text me when and where to meet and I'll be there.*

A few moments later, Zac's response appears on my screen...and it makes me roll my eyes so hard I think I may have strained an eyeball.

The thumbs-up emoji? Is he kidding?

Suffice to say the smile that was encroaching on my hairline has gone south at this point. I'm not a trend watcher and I'm certainly not what I call cool, but even I know that replying with a thumbs-up emoji can be a kiss of death. Not worth a smiley face and we're not at the point where he can give me a heart, these are the parts of emoji talk which I speak. But a thumbs-up?

I'm still working out its meaning when I open my car door and climb out. Riley and Amelia, who had been chatting at the picnic table by the kitchen, have both hopped up to come greet me.

"You okay?" Riley's brow is furrowed with concern.

Nodding my head, I give each woman a quick hug. "Me? I'm fine. Why would you ask?"

Amelia squints her eyes and places her hands on her hips as she takes me in. "Cause you look like you just smelled something bad."

"Oh, no." I wave a hand in the air, pushing away my little white lie. "I mean, I've got a lot on my mind, but that's not why we're here."

Turning our attention to Amelia, Riley waves her phone

in the air. "What's up with your cryptic message this morning, Amelia?"

We have a group chat with all of us—me, Riley, Dylan, and Amelia—on it. I've been loving it that Dylan keeps us updated on her travels by treating us to photos and the occasional voice text, but this morning's message from Amelia had me worried.

"Waking up to a text that says 'Hi. Don't ask me any questions, just come over when you can. Thanks.' leaves a lot up to our imaginations." I put an arm around her shoulders. "Are *you* okay?"

"Look, I don't want to make a big deal out of things, but Spencer and I decided to officially separate at the end of this year."

I'm pretty sure I'm going to have a bruise on my jaw from the force with which it hit the floor. When I look at Riley, I find her with her mouth in the same position.

"Please. Don't." Amelia holds a hand up before either one of us can utter a syllable. "I have a lot of unpacking to do around this, and I know I'll need all of you by my side later in the year when this becomes reality, but right now it's about something else."

Locking eyes with Riley, I can see she is as full of questions as I am. I drag my gaze slowly over to Amelia, who stands with her arms wrapped around her middle looking tired and sad, but also like a weight's been lifted. I know her well enough to know part of this is an act; she'll be stoic and pretend everything is okay until she's forced to handle it, and as her friend, I intend to do whatever it is she needs me to do to help her through it.

Even if it means we can't really discuss "it" right now.

"Okay, then you tell us when you do want to talk about it and we'll make a pact now that we're here for you, okay?"

Riley, who sometimes ignores what people want because

she's a hugger, is already enveloping Amelia in her arms. She hugs her close for a mere second before stepping away.

"Sorry." Sheepishly she rocks her eyes back and forth between Amelia and myself. "I had to."

"It's okay." Amelia chuckles. "And you don't need to tip-toe around me, it's life. And..." She takes a big breath, hiking her shoulders up with it as she does, and releasing it in a whoosh. "Well, Spencer and I were going over our shared properties and possessions and all that stuff, and we made a decision about the small businesses we want to put here on the campground."

I feel my gut hitch. I had so hoped my wine shop would be one of those small businesses that Amelia speaks of, but thanks to my issues with Steve, I've had to stick that thought away until he and I solve our problems.

Riley scratches her head. "Are you splitting up the campground between the two of you?"

"No." Amelia shakes her head as she pulls a set of keys out of her pocket. "He's going to keep the art gallery, cause he loves it, and I'm taking over the Sweetkiss Creek Campground, because it's my baby."

"That's...great?" I put one hand in the air to cheer, and stick the other one out questioningly at my side. I'm not sure if we're supposed to be happy or upset for Amelia right now; I just want to do the right thing.

"It's what it is, but..." She steps forward and takes my hand that's high in the air cheering and pulls it down. She flips it over, uncurls my fingers, and places the key ring in the palm of my hand. "...I've wanted to just give you that space to use since you showed interest in it. Spencer wanted to keep it and not rent it out, only because he wanted to be sure we were keeping the buildings. Now that I'm taking over, he doesn't have to worry about the buildings."

I stare at the set of keys in my hand. They're all silver and gold keys, except for one lone key that's been painted with hearts and unicorns on it.

I hold it up. "Why are you giving me these keys?"

"Because I want you to open your wine shop or tasting room or whatever it's going to be." Amelia claps her hands together as she throws her head back and laughs. "I want you to have the freedom you need right now to pick yourself up by your bootstraps and start over. I hate seeing you tied up like this because of some fictitious lawsuit your ex is holding over you for no good reason."

Not sure what to do or think, I can only stare at the keys in my hand, that is until the wet from tears clouds my vision.

A lone tear breaks the dam and starts its solo journey down my cheek. Riley flicks out a tissue from her purse and dabs my cheek.

"Don't start crying, cause then I'll have to cry." She clucks, turning to Amelia. "I feel like it's our job as her friends to cry with her, right?"

When Amelia doesn't speak, I glance up to find her studying me with tears in her eyes. "Since the day I met you, you've been nothing but kind to me." She reaches out and grabs Riley's hand at the same time she takes mine and squeezes it. "I didn't have an easy life growing up, so I never knew that I would go out in the world and find family. But you two, and Dylan, have shown me what true family is. It's not the people we share blood with, it's those who we pick to be on our team."

The three of us huddle together, standing in a circle with our heads touching and still holding hands, all of us sniffling. Amelia's the one who breaks away first, waving her hands in the air and calling an emotional time-out.

"Okay, one thing I promised myself was that I was going to keep a cheerful outlook no matter what this year, so let's get you inside your new place of business and start making plans, shall we?"

Wiping tears from her cheeks, Riley jumps in the air and squeals. "We're gonna have a new wine bar to hang out in!"

"Unless she hires you to work for her." Amelia looks at me. "Has she told you she wants to quit the cafe?"

With the cafe being her family's business, it's hard to think about Riley not working there, but also knowing how unhappy she's been, it makes sense. "She's not mentioned it. Yet."

"'She'll tell you more soon," Riley says, sticking her tongue out at us. "Since I'm the 'she' you're referring to, that is. Right now, it's all about you." With a whoop of joy, Riley swipes the keys from my hand and sprints ahead of us, opening the door.

"Come on!" She's loud, excited, and off-the-charts happy. Luckily, as I catch Amelia laughing, it's infectious.

"Hey." I grab Amelia's arm before we go inside. "Seriously, how much do you want for rent?"

"We'll figure that out once we get you in here." She threads her arm through mine. "I don't like seeing someone being held back from doing something they love and want to do because of something stupid. If you need to open this and use the space rent-free for the next two years, then so be it."

"This is too much, it's so kind of you, Amelia. I would hate for anyone to think I was taking advantage of anything."

"Advantage? Are you kidding me?" Amelia snorts. "You do realize my husband makes a lot of money, right? Trust me, I'll be fine."

As she pulls her arm from mine, she turns around one last time to give me another hug, then skips ahead and joins Riley inside the space. Standing on the old porch outside and looking in, I watch my two friends as they dance around and sing Broadway tunes at the top of their lungs.

And I count my blessings.

When I pull into my driveway later that evening, my mind is focused on getting inside so I can let the dogs out. Plus, it's Sunday night, and to me that's a night to hang out and take care of yourself. I love having downtime and a quiet night in on a Sunday because I feel like it gears me up for the week ahead.

As I put my car into park, I lean back in my seat and do a happy dance. I can't wait to tell Zac when I see him that my dream to open the tasting room is going to come true. And, as I told Amelia before I left, if it kills me, I want to start paying her rent as soon as I open. I don't know how, but I'll find a way to make things work until I can settle things with Steve.

I get out of the car and immediately my mind races to decorating the retail space. There's so much I need to do before I can think about opening, and I'm so caught up in my planning it's no wonder I don't see Steve sitting on my front porch.

I'm halfway up the porch steps when he announces his presence.

"Hey, Etta."

TWENTY-ONE

Etta

Startled, I grab at my heart when he manages to scare me mid-step. Ever the graceful goddess that I am, I don't even fight gravity as it tugs on me. Instead, I go with the flow. I know if I try to fight a fall like this, I'm going to end up with splinters or stitches, and neither sounds like fun at the moment.

Luckily, I ended up on my back. Pretty sure I look like a turtle who's been flipped onto his shell. I keep my eyes pinched closed, not because I'm hurt, but because I'm so irritated that Steve is the one who's done this to me. I want to scream.

"Are you okay?" he asks from his chair. It's like him to not even get up.

Sitting up, I pull a few bright red maple leaves from my hair and wipe the grass off my cheek. "I'm peachy. And how are you this fine evening?" I begin to stand up, slowly, raising myself up vertebrae by vertebrae. "Oh, no, Steve. Please do not help me. I can't stand it when you're so good to me."

"Oh, man..." As if someone's lit a fire under his butt, he's suddenly up and off his chair, hand outstretched like he wants to help.

Too little, too late. It's no wonder we split.

I snap my arm away from his grasp, a little too roughly. Feeling somewhat bad, I look at him apologetically and point to the chairs for us to sit.

"So," I begin, taking my seat. "You obviously have something important to say to end up here waiting for me in the dark. Like an owl."

"I started to leave and drive back today, but it didn't feel right."

"Being of sound mind, I can say that the reason you don't feel good is because your heart is dark and icy. I'm pretty sure it's pumping dust."

"I always wondered why you didn't want to work for a greeting card company," Steve says in an attempt to tease me.

Looking at my front door, I'm reminded there are two dogs who need to get out. I hop up and pull out my keys, unlocking the door and opening it wide enough to let Thor and Hercules out. They burst through, beelining it to Steve to say hello before racing out to do their business in the yard.

"Okay, what can I do for you before we get you on the road?" I ask as I sit back down. The rumble in my stomach tells us both it's time for me to eat.

"I'm here to let you know I'm dropping all of it." His eyes are downcast, and he won't make eye contact with me. "I spoke to my lawyer yesterday and asked him to stop it all."

"I guess you finally realized that you could get into a lot of trouble for your lawsuit?"

Steve shrugs. "I did get an earful from my lawyer about frivolous lawsuits. And he told me that you could decide to sue me for malicious prosecution. Our judge is going to decide this week if he's going to fine me for taking up his time with this case."

I can tell by looking at him that he's feeling as defeated right now as I do vindicated. I don't want to tell him that I won't press charges. He doesn't get that satisfaction. Not yet. "Why did you do it, Steve?"

"Call me crazy, but for a period of time after we split I thought we'd get back together." He throws a lopsided grin my way. "I know you're here and happy now, I've seen it for myself. Even that guy you're dating, Zeke..."

"Zac." I roll my eyes, but can't help a giggle.

"Whatever. Seeing you with someone else made it real, that you have moved on." With a shake of his head, he stands up. "I've already started the process of having that money transferred back to you for your part of the business. And, this"—he reaches around and pulls a folded-up piece of paper out of his back pocket, unfolding it to show me the non-compete clause—"is outta here."

With a flourish, he grabs the paper and pulls it apart, shredding it into two pieces. The night air suddenly chills my skin, a faint breeze licking my ankles. Across the lawn, Thor and Herc race in a circle, with Thor stopping to pee on Steve's car. Karma.

I'd spent the better part of the last few months in shock and being hurt by this man and his lawsuit, I'll be honest I'm not sure what to feel right now. But for the moment, I'm going to settle on relief.

"Wow." I take a breath of air and sigh it out slowly. "I'm glad you're letting it go, Steve. Part of me feels like I should say thank you, but another part of me is still really, really mad at you for even putting me through the stress."

Steve walks over and stands in front of me, watching me. I pull my eyes to his, and I swear I can still see stormy weather circling. But if it is, one thing's for sure: it's not my problem anymore.

"Well." He shoves his hands in his pockets and inclines his

chin toward his car. "I'm gonna get going. I had to let you know my decision and I really wanted to say I'm sorry one more time. It was screwed up, controlling, and immature of me to do. All because I wanted things to go my way."

"It takes a big person to admit something like that, Steve." I stand as well, crossing my arms in front of me like a wall. I walk with him to his car, my stomach still rumbling. "Thanks for being man enough to tell me all of this to my face. If you had texted me about this..."

"...you'd have killed me." He chuckles, his head down as he climbs behind the wheel of his rental car. "Take care of yourself, Etta, okay?"

"Drive safe." I start the walk back up to my porch, but then turn around and flag Steve to stop before he pulls all the way out of the drive. I motion for him to roll down his window. "Also, for the record, I won't sue you for malicious anything, Steve. Let's just leave it here, okay?"

With that, he smiles, looking away at the road in front of him before he pulls his eyes back to mine. With a flick of his wrist, he waves as he puts his car in drive and disappears out of sight.

Taking a moment in my yard, I stretch my body out, reaching to the sky, then dropping my hands to the ground, folding my body over and feeling it stretch and pull and tug the tension away. Mental note: I need to hit a yoga class this week, especially before that dance next weekend.

Thinking of the dance makes me think of Zac, which makes me smile. I whistle for the dogs and we head up the steps back into the house. I'm in my head wondering about what to wear next week when my stomach rumbles so loudly, Thor barks which sets off Hercules.

At this moment, I remember I have no groceries, and therefore nothing to eat. So, opening the door, I let them back in and shut it behind them. My purse is still in the car, so I lock the door, again, and jog to my car. A quick trip to the local burger joint would do me good tonight, or at least tide me over until I can run to the store tomorrow.

Unfortunately, Sunday night around Sweetkiss Creek means almost everything is closed up. I point my car toward the interstate, knowing that the closer I get to it, the more options I'll find for food. In ten minutes, I'm not disappointed; I pull up outside an old highway truck stop that has it all. There's a small grocery store, a diner that flashes an "Open twenty-four hours, seven days a week!" sign, a pizza place, and two fast food joints. Gauging the options, I pick the pizza place figuring I can have dinner and breakfast, all with one pizza.

I wander inside and place my order and am told to wait in the lobby until they call my name. The pizza place is an interesting setup with the lobby being in a side room with a television and a couple of sofas.

The teenager working behind the cash register must have seen the look on my face. "It used to be a room for truckers to take naps in when they were on the road."

"They'd order food, then sleep it off?"

The kid nods, arranging his baseball cap on his head so it sits better. "You can hang there until your food's ready. There's a remote for the TV, too."

Left to my own devices, and all alone in the lobby, I opt to mute the television and sit and relax. There's been enough going on the last few weeks; I don't need any more distractions.

Just on the other side from where I'm perched, I can hear a low murmur of conversation. I settled back in my chair, a fan of eavesdropping. I know...it's a terrible habit, but I see it as a hobby. I can listen to someone I don't know talk and then make up stories about them in my mind. If you've never done it, I'm going to highly suggest that you do it at least once. It's so much fun.

From what I can tell, it sounds like there's two tables on the other side of the wall from me. One could be a mother and son—it sounds like she's encouraging him to try out for the school football team, but if I'm not mistaken, he's trying to get her to wrap her head around the fact he wants to do theater. Clutching my heart, I lean closer to the wall, hoping the faceless kid I've never met will get a chance to fulfill his dream of starring in the high school version of *South Pacific* and singing "Some Enchanted Evening" with his friends. Theater kids are the best.

The other table sounds like a couple of guys. When I overhear one challenging the other in a race to eat the hottest chicken wings, I get really curious. I find myself scooting over closer to the other end of the wall so I can hear more of this particular conversation. Not that I don't like a good musical, but a couple of dudes challenging each other to do stupid things like eating the hottest wings can only end one way: hilariously.

"Excuse me," a guy we'll call Man A says, who must be flagging down a waitress, because the next thing I hear is, "Can you bring us each one dozen of your hottest wings?"

Man B groans. "Are you serious with this? I thought you were joking."

"If there's one thing I won't do, it's joke when it comes to competition. You can ask anyone."

Man A sounds like a pain, but he's also the livewire of these two. You know how every now and then you'll be scrolling social media and World's Stupidest Moments pops up as a post from some random account? You know the one: you see things like people not paying attention to where they're walking cause they're on their phone, so they fall in a pool or run into a pole and hit their head.

Well, I get the feeling that Man A is one of these types, and much like a good train wreck, well...I gotta stay and see it, yeah?

"I'd love to ask someone you know about how your mind works," Man B chortles. "Cause it's a mystery to most of us at work."

"I'm in a zone when I look at things as a competition." A's voice sounds like he's quite proud of himself. "My brother and I have always been like this. It's our biggest weakness and our greatest strength."

I roll my eyes. Yeah, dude. Being uber-competitive is a fabulous strength, I bet the ladies love it. I catch my sarcastic thought and give myself a gentle rattle, laughing at my crankiness. That's not who I want to be. I'm sure Man A isn't all that bad...even if it is fun to laugh at him from the other side of a wall.

"You call the way you act when we have team building events a strength?" Man B howls with laughter. "You're crazy! Our supervisor wanted you off the team because your participation level is so extra."

Man A is quiet; I can imagine he's the kind of guy who needs to walk back statements most of his life. So, I scoot closer to the wall so I can hear what's next.

"It's not extra when you want to win! Plus, it's ingrained in me, I can't get away from it. It's like an addiction."

Man B is still cracking up. "Tuck," he says with a snort, "you just told me that you made a bet with your brother for a baseball card. Who does that?"

I'm loving this. I hold back my own snort, thinking about two brothers making some kind of ridiculous stupid bet over a baseball card.

"Who does that?" A sounds offended. "I'll tell you who does that, another competitive man who wants to fulfill his baseball card collection. As soon as my brother realized he would finally get the last baseball card he needs to complete his collection, you can bet he said yes."

Shaking my head, I'm startled when the intercom comes on in the small room. "McCoy, your order's ready. McCoy, pizza is ready."

I make my way out of the room and over to the cashier stand. I wait while my teenage friend puts the finishing touches on my pizza and places it in its cardboard box. As I wait, I'm ridiculously excited I can still hear Man A chatting away to his annoyed work colleague. I'm half tempted to sit here and eat my pizza so I can find out what happens with their wing challenge, but another rumble from my belly tells me I'm gonna want to get home with my hot pizza and fast.

"So..." Man B must have gotten something to eat because it sounds like he's speaking in between bites. "You bet your brother he couldn't get a date with some girl in the small town where he's a cop?"

Huh. That's interesting.

"Oh, it's more to it than that, Daniel." Man A stops to take a swig of his drink.

"What do you mean?" asks B.

"He's been stuck with her on a double date before, and apparently, she's hot but a pain in the arse."

Did he really just say arse? My hands rise up and grip the counter.

"Specifics. C'mon."

I nod my head in agreement with Man B. We need specifics, Man A. Speak up, please.

"Okay, specifics. Well, on their double date, they went to an escape room and they didn't get along. Like pickles and peanut butter. He said she was trying to be commanding, telling everybody what to do, and it rubbed him the wrong way. And look, he's the kind of person who won't say anything bad about anyone, but he did call her complex and complicated."

I look down, surprised to find my knuckles white. Didn't realize I was clenching so strongly.

"So, she's bold and your bro couldn't handle it?"

I'm liking Man B more and more.

"Don't know," replies Man A. "He's mentioned pulling her over and having to arrest her..."

My skin suddenly prickles. There are some strong similarities here that I'm beginning to question.

"What?" Man B is incredulous, and I feel a stab at my heart. "He arrested her?"

"Yeah, and also—this is funny—her dog keeps running away from her. Guess where he goes? To the police station where Zac works. At least once a week, he said."

The two men are laughing at the same time a flume of icy-cold fluid blasts through my body. Man A's brother is Zac?

Zac made a bet with his brother that he could ask me out?

The only reason Zac asked me out was so he could win a baseball card?

I'm in such a state of shock that I grab my keys and walk out to my car and open the door to get inside, leaving the pizza on the counter. It's not until I'm turning the key in the ignition, about to put my car in reverse, when the teenager who took my order appears at the driver's side window. I came here to get food, and while my stomach may be rumbling, it's pretty fair to say I'm not hungry now.

Shaking, I take the pizza from this nice kid, but not before warning him to be kind to women or I'd come back and haunt him. I toss it on the floor of the passenger's side and pull out of the parking lot, headed home. All of the light and happiness I'd been feeling when I pulled in here half an hour ago is gone. Wiped away.

Zac Wright is a ding-dong devil and I'm gonna kill him, and kill him good, when I get ahold of him.

TWENTY-TWO

Zac

Monday mornings are always the hardest for me to get out of bed. Today is no different. After a weekend of trying to corner Etta alone so I could explain to her about the bet, my cowardice in asking her out, and let her know I really do want to go on a date with her... well, I'm mentally worn out.

Dubs has a fresh pot of coffee ready when I stop by to pick up his bill before work. I stay long enough to pour myself a cup, holding it tight as he places the invoice in my free hand.

"So." As if he could read my mind, the older man pokes me in my side. "Have you told her yet?"

I can't make eye contact at first. Instead, I slowly move my head side to side, in a negative way. When I finally glance up, Dubs's concerned look makes my stomach hitch.

He lets out a long exhale of air. "You're gonna mess this up, Wright. I'm telling you now because I'm watching it happen."

He's right. I know he's right as much as he knows he's right. "I tried all weekend to get her alone. I even had a chance to tell her, but she was in such a good mood I didn't want to ruin things."

"You call her now and tell her you're coming over after work. It's that simple."

Easy for the person to say who isn't the one in trouble. "She's going to be furious with me."

"Furious? That may be a bit dramatic," Dubs says with a laugh. "She may be peeved at first, but if your intention is real, then she'll figure it out."

"Dubs, I've never met anyone like her in my life." Running my fingers through my hair, I fight the urge to tug on the strands. "She makes me crazy, spinning like a top and out-of-control crazy, but then she says something that makes me laugh."

"And I bet you laugh with her like you've never laughed with anyone else...am I right?"

I hold my thumb and forefinger together in the air. "Little bit."

"If memory serves me, you two met and didn't get along."

Chuckling, I put my coffee down and shove my hands in my pockets. "No, we didn't. After that first meeting, she would cross the street if she saw me coming. I once caught her hiding behind a bread display at the grocery store, just so she didn't have to walk past me. She has no clue I saw her, though."

"Oh, young love." Dubs chortles, his phone going off in his pocket. "Believe it or not, but these are the days you'll look back on fondly...long after you two are married."

Dubs's phone goes off again.

I point to his pocket. "You need to get that?"

"I'll look to see who it is in a sec; I'm busy talking to you." He grins as the phone beeps again. "So. What are you gonna do to fix things?"

"I'm going to call her and make a plan to see her tonight."

"Perfect." As his phone chimes one more time, the old man looks to the ceiling. "For the love of...who is trying to get ahold of me?"

Ignoring Dubs as he mutters to his phone, I pace the room, repeating myself. "I am going to tell Etta the truth. Tonight, I will see her and tell her that while my asking her out may have started as a bet, it's turned into more for me..."

Dubs holds his hand up. "But, Zac, wait,—"

Shaking my head, I won't let him interrupt. "No, it has turned into more. And I want her to know so she can get it through that thick skull of hers I only took the bet to date her..."

"Remember I told you I put in those security cameras so I'd be alerted on my phone when someone was on the property? Well, I think you should hit pause and maybe..."

"Dubs," I say, spinning around to face him. "I can't hit pause. She's going to think the only reason I asked her on a date is so I can win a baseball card from my brother. Who does that?"

As the last word trips out of my mouth, Dubs dips his head and holds up his phone. I take a step forward to look at what he's showing me on his screen. The video isn't the best quality, but I see a figure in a striped sweater standing outside the doorway of the room I'm in, right now, with Dubs.

Recognition hits me square in the stomach as Dubs lowers his eyes to the floor.

Behind me, a voice pipes up at the same time the figure on the screen steps into the room with us.

"Yeah." Etta is seething, her voice drawn and on edge, straightening her striped sweater as she walks up to where I stand. "Who does that?"

Etta paces the garage bay slowly. I'd managed to talk her into listening to me and not taking off and leaving, like she wanted to do. Dubs had even closed up shop and left, giving us complete privacy from him and from any possible clients popping in.

"Can I explain what happened?" My palms are slick with anxiety perspiration, not excited perspiration. "I've been trying to talk to you about this for a few days now."

Etta stops and puts one hand on her hip, cocking her head to one side and looking at me with narrowed eyes. "You should have tried harder."

She's right. All I can do is agree with her, so I nod. "I could have, but I didn't want to. We were having such a nice time when we had coffee the other day, I didn't want to ruin it. I'd promised Brett and Lane I would…"

"What?" Etta's head almost snaps off its axis. "They know, too? Great. Makes my embarrassment much more amazing. Now I'm the fool in two towns."

I'm not going to lie: I'm sick to my stomach over the whole thing. I should have known this would be the outcome. Or at least prepared for it better than I have.

"You're not a fool," I say, shoving my hands in my pockets. Hands that want to reach out and pull her close to me right now, but I can't. "I'm the fool. I'm the village idiot for doing this to you."

Etta stands facing the street, her arms folded in front of her, leaving me to plead with her backside.

"I'm sorry, Etta, I really am." I take a tentative step toward her. "Does it help to know that I want to go out with you, that I really did want there to be a date with you?"

Silence.

I take another step forward.

"Think about it. When we met, we didn't get along. We

haven't gotten along since I came to town, but I've thought about you—and nothing but you—since I moved here."

"You're only saying that because my dog kept showing up at your work."

At least she's talking to me. I don't want to get too excited, but I feel positive. I take another step closer to her.

"True. But it also gave me a chance to get your number, since I had to let you know where Thor was." I swallow the lump in my throat. "Please, Etta. Turn around and let me find a way to make this up to you."

We stand here for a few more seconds before she begins to slowly spin in place, turning to face me. And the look on her face breaks my heart.

"Do you want to know how I found out?" She asks it as a question, but I know it's not. "I was at the truck stop near Taylortown and I overheard your brother talking to someone about how he bet his brother a baseball card he could go out with some girl."

I want to get mad and blame Tuck—he's an easy target to use right now. But the fact is, I'm the one who took the bet, so all I can do is stand here and take everything I deserve.

Etta may be talking to me, but she won't look at me... which breaks my heart. All I want is to dive into those teal-blue eyes of hers, but she keeps them downcast, staring at the concrete floor.

"You never should have heard about the bet like that, not that I ever should have made a bet." I reach out to touch her arm, and she shrinks away. I may have taken three steps forward to meet her, but I feel like this is going to chuck us ten steps back.

She holds her arm where my hand almost grazed her skin, as if protecting herself from my touch. "No, there never should have been a bet. I know I was grumpy, Zac. I've been grumpy and cranky and really put off toward people for a few months."

I open my mouth to agree, but she holds up a finger. "Let me finish."

Nodding my head, I stand back and clasp my hands, listening.

"My ex really did a number on me as far as trust goes, and I told you that. I've been working really hard on myself so I can be happy—to think about dating again without being worried the other person is going to try to manipulate me or take something from me when and if it ends." She shakes her head, chuckling at herself. "Do you know how hard it is to change your own mind?"

"As someone who has gone through his own self-help phase, yes. I do."

"So why did you do it, then? Why take the bet when you knew in your heart, and after getting to know me, that you're dealing with a vulnerable woman?"

Ouch. "When you put it like that..."

She rolls her eyes and throws her hands toward the sky. "I shouldn't have to put it any way to anyone." She taps her head. "You should have thought about it, Zac. That's why this hurts so much."

"Please believe me that I was trying to tell you about this all weekend. I really was and never had a chance to..."

"Stop." She grabs her car keys out of her pocket and folds her arms in front of her chest again. "I actually cannot hear any more of this right now."

"Okay, then can I come over after work tonight? I can bring some food and we can talk."

Etta shakes her head. "I'm painting."

"I'll come help." I shove my fingers through my hair, desperate to keep her in front of me. "Even if it's cleaning up."

"That's okay." She glances at her watch. "I need to get

going; the dogs have a vet appointment and I literally would rather watch paint dry than continue this conversation."

She spins on her heel and starts marching to the door, and my heart drops to my feet.

"Etta, wait," I say as I reach out and touch her shoulder. "Please."

She shudders as she stops, but she stops. She stands with her back to me, only turning her head so I can see the side of her face.

"What do you want?"

"I want you to know I really am so, so, very sorry." When she doesn't move, I inch closer and drop my voice down a notch. "I needed a kick in the butt to ask you out, okay? You kinda scared me when we met, but the more I was around you, the more I needed to get to know you. Then I kissed you and everything blew apart inside me, as if you were the glue that was here to put me back together. I. Am. Sorry. And I'll tell you that every day for the rest of our lives if you'll let me."

Her eyes focus on the floor as she swallows. I watch her shoulders rise and fall as she takes a breath, and I fight the urge to pull her close to my chest and run my lips up and down her neck.

As I wait for her to respond, we're both surprised when a couple of men wearing T+T Auto Parts uniforms fling the main door to the office open. "Yo, Dubs. Where you at? We've got your delivery here."

Making eye contact with one of the guys, they wave an invoice in the air at me. Realizing I need to go find Dubs so he can handle this, I look to Etta so I can explain. But she's already got her hand on the door handle and is on her way out.

"Etta, wait," I call out.

She waves a hand at me, but doesn't look back. "We'll talk later."

It's not good enough. I know I am the last person who

should be making demands, but I can't have her leaving here mad. "Look, I don't give a toss about that baseball card. I want you, okay? You're the only reason I took the bet."

Behind me one of the delivery men clears his throat. "So, can you get Dubs for us?"

I hold up a hand to the guy. "One sec."

Running to the door, I watch as she makes her way down the sidewalk to her car. She opens her driver's side door and starts to get in.

"Etta." I wait for her to pause so I don't look completely insane screaming down the street. "Please believe me. All I wanted was a date with you. Only you."

I don't know if she's even listening to me because she gets in the car and slams the door shut. I watch as she pulls out of her spot and drives past me and down the street.

I just hope she's not driving out of my life.

TWENTY-THREE

Etta

Ever since I was little, I've had a habit of digging into a project when things take over—you know, when the world as you know it spins out of control and you have no way to rein it in. That kind of habit. I think it's always worked for me because it keeps my mind occupied and I can stop thinking about whatever it is that I'm upset about.

But that was before I had an Amelia and a Riley in my life. Dylan, too, who may be absent, but her phone call last night to cheer me up was not overlooked.

My phone chimes on the coffee table. Riley sits closest to it and grabs it, showing me the screen.

"Another text from Zac." She nudges my elbow with the tip of the phone. "Are you going to respond? That's like, the tenth message he's sent you and I've only been here for an hour."

"Ten is a little exaggerated." My arms are in midair as I glide my paint roller over the hallway walls. "I feel like four is a more ladylike number."

"Ladylike?" Amelia grunts as she hops down from the stool she's been balancing on. "I think it would be ladylike for you to hire painters to do this. Doesn't someone know a teenager we can coerce into painting your house?"

"Not if I want it done right." Standing back, I inspect our work so far. "Okay, second coat in the hallway is done!"

"Good timing." Riley waves a few menus in the air. "I'm starving. My treat if I can get you two to come with me to grab some dinner?"

Amelia says yes at the same time I shake my head no. Both women give me a look of despair.

"Don't do that with your faces, you guys. I'm fine. I'm not as angry as I was, so rest assured I won't be pulling out my flame thrower and tracking down Zac tonight."

"Thank goodness, because I borrowed your flamethrower and haven't given it back yet." Riley's attempt to make me smile works, but just barely. "If you don't want to come with us, can we bring you food back?"

Shaking my head again, I use my chin to point to the fridge. "I'm stocked up. But thank you. You two—especially you, Riley—should think about going home."

Riley had come over and basically moved in after I told her what happened a few days ago. I think she broke a land-speed record driving to my place cause she lives about ten minutes away and I swear she was here in less than two.

"I'm happy to stay another night, too. I'm a firm believer that no one should be alone in a time of crisis." She says this to Amelia, but we all know she's talking about me.

"Or you could be trying to avoid being at your parents now that you've told them you're quitting...that couldn't be it, right?" Amelia queries, tossing a wink my way.

"Shh. Let's not talk about that and the fact they want me to move out next month." Riley rolls her eyes. "I knew this would happen."

"You're being independent. So what, you don't want to go

into the family business." I throw an arm around Riley's shoulders. "It will all work out."

"We'll see." Riley grabs her purse and digs through it, finding her keys. She looks at me before rocking her eyes to the phone, which she's put back on the coffee table. "You and Zac...will it all work out?"

Sighing, I sit down in my favorite chair and stare out the front window. Do I want things to work out for me and Zac? Oddly enough, yes. If someone would have told me even two weeks ago that I would have that thought, I would have called them a liar. Then slapped them for good measure.

"He lays out why he took the bet in the last email he sent you." Amelia stands by the front door with her arms crossed. "I'm the one out of all of us who should be the most jaded, since I'm the one who's getting separated, but even I can read between those lines."

Besides assaulting my phone with a bevy of text messages asking for me to forgive him, Zac had also sent me two emails. One was nothing but "I'm sorry" and other apologies. I give him credit, though: he did say he was sorry in French, Italian, and Spanish as well in those emails so...points to you, Zac.

The second email was longer, and in this one he repeated what he had told me when I last saw him in person. That one does explain his reasons why he did what he did, but I'm not ashamed to say my ego is still bruised and my feelings are hurt.

But there's another feeling I have about Zac and this situation—and I'm not sure what it is yet. I want to put my finger on it, but I guess I'll have to wait for it to reveal itself.

"He can write all the emails and texts he wants right now, but I need time to get over it." I shrug a shoulder and let it drop limply. "I *think* I do. I'm really not sure, you guys. I was falling for him...no. It's more than that."

"What do you mean, it's more?" Riley moves over to kneel beside my chair.

How do I say I was finally starting to trust him and trust myself? Trust saying yes and I, oh boy, I even trusted his kiss. Not that I had to trust the kiss, but it was the meaning and the expectation of what was behind that kiss.

My hand flies to my mouth, and I allow my fingertips to dance along my lips, re-tracing where Zac's kisses had fallen only days ago.

"I think she's trying to say she fell for him." Amelia reaches out and squeezes my shoulder. "Fair assessment?"

Nodding, I put my hand over hers and drag my eyes to meet Riley's. "She's right. I fell hard, too."

Riley bends down and throws her arms around me at the same time Amelia does it as well. Me, I let them both smother me with friendship and strength, cause I'm running low on motivation today.

"Okay, we'll go get food, but I'm coming back and staying over another night." Riley takes her forefinger and taps my nose on the very tip, doing her best Alexis from *Schitt's Creek* impersonation. "Boop."

"Get outta here." I swat at her hand, laughing. "Stay as long as you like. I got a three-bedroom for a reason, you know."

"I'm so glad you said that," Riley calls out over her shoulder as she walks out the front door. "Be back soon!"

"You know she's going to ask you to move in here, right?" Amelia manages to get out before she's dragged out the front door.

Laughing, I stare at the closed door for a few minutes, almost expecting one of them to come back in for a last performance. Having the two of them around has been awesome, but it doesn't allow time for me to get in my head. I learned a long time ago from my therapist that the mind is a dangerous neighborhood...you never want to go in it alone. Makes sense.

Hearing my tummy growl, I head into the kitchen to heat

up some leftovers. As soon as I open the refrigerator, two small dogs appear at my feet like magic. No one is safe in a ten-mile radius around these parts if they open anything with a plastic top. These two are there, expecting to share whatever it is you've got.

Once I get the food going in the microwave, I walk Thor and Hercules to the front door so they can go out and do their business. Only, as I open it, they take off running down the drive. Parked at the end is a small sports car and a well-dressed man is climbing out of it on the driver's side. They circle him, following him as he makes his way toward me.

"Can I help you?"

"Are you Etta McCoy?"

"I am."

"I'm Zac's brother. It seems you and I need to have a talk about my big mouth."

"Ahhhhh." Recognition takes over when he speaks. "You're the man from the truck stop the other night, the one talking so loud I was able to hear every word he said. The man who loves to compete with his brother."

"Also known as Tuck." Stopping at the bottom of the porch steps, Tuck shoves his hands in his pockets. "I'm here to say I'm sorry. I'm the one who had the idea for him to ask you out."

"Just because it was your idea doesn't mean he had to say yes, does it?"

Tuck grins. "I like how you think, McCoy."

Crossing my arms in front of me, I look him up and down, from the bottom of his feet to the top of his head. I make sure he knows I'm doing it, too.

"You sizing me up?"

"Making sure I can take you out if I need to," I tease. Turning around, I head inside. "Cup of coffee?"

"So you two have been essentially in competition since you were little?"

Tuck nods, taking a sip of his coffee. "It's sad but true. When you grow up like we did, you try to find ways to entertain yourself. I think we both have competitive personalities, but the fact it was encouraged doesn't help."

"What do you mean when you say 'growing up like you did?'"

"Well, our grandfather was governor and our mom's a bit of a big-deal lawyer. We had nannies, tutors, and were expected to do as we were told to do, not to do as our parents did...if that makes sense?"

"Totally. I take it because of the public eye being on you guys so much, you were kept insular?"

"Yep. We had each other to hang out with until we were finally shipped off to boarding school. Look, I was always jealous of Zac. I spent a lot of time taking things from him: toys, parts in school plays..."

"Ouch. You did?"

"Oh, I did. He wanted Robin Hood, but I won it from him, fair and square. We once bet on a car..."

"What?" I can't even control my shock. "A car?"

"I'll just say I loved that old Ford Focus with all of my heart." Tuck's cheeks flash bright red. "Look, Zac isn't me. I'm pushy and always want to win. It's why I ended up following in my mother's footsteps and became a lawyer."

It's not like I don't want to admit it, but wow. I'm starting to understand the way these Wright boys think. And that is scary.

Tuck reaches into his back pocket and pulls out a small card, holding it in the air. "This is the baseball card in question."

"And you won it?" Taking it from his hands, I flip it over and look at its front and back.

"Yeah." He snickers. "I won it, and the first thing I did was lord it over my brother and then use it to get him to play a game with me."

"I could see that," I say, handing the card back. "But it's something that bonds you two. I can't deny it's weird that at your age you still get so crazy about competing with him, but I'm not here to judge anyone."

"Yet, you have every right to judge me because it was my suggestion to use you as the bet. And for that, I am happy to spend as much time as I need saying I'm sorry to you."

The whole time we've sat here, I've watched Tuck. I can see his sincerity and feel his apology, if apologies are things we can feel. It's funny how I can see Zac in his movements and hear him in the inflection of his tone, too. Brothers. Family.

Coming from a family with two brothers myself, I'm starting to really get it. Tuck sitting here, talking to me is soooo familiar. There are things I've done for my family, especially for my twin, Jack, that I needed to do. I still pat myself on the back and take total credit for getting him together—FINALLY—with the love of his life.

As his sister, I firmly believe that if I hadn't interfered, they wouldn't be married today. Now, looking at Zac's brother sitting here in front of me, telling me his side of things and attempting to put me in the picture, I can't help but wonder if I need to give this guy a chance. The same way I begged someone to give my brother a chance not so long ago.

"I think you can stop saying it now." I'm surprised my voice comes out so low, barely a whisper. "Tuck, you're forgiven. And thank you for coming here to tell me in person."

Tuck puts his coffee mug down on the side table. "You mean it?"

I shrug my shoulders and smile. "I do."

Tuck stands, petting both dogs at his feet before he does. "He really likes you, Etta, and I'm not just saying that."

Looking into Tuck's eyes, I can see he's telling the truth. I squeeze his arm as we walk in tandem to the front door. "Thank you for coming here tonight. How did you find me, anyway?"

"Small towns." Tuck chuckles. "I called the police station and explained to Lane what I wanted to do, so he told me where Thor lives."

"Ah." Glancing over my shoulder, I see my escape artist as he settles in his dog bed by the fireplace for the night. "I need to talk to Lane about privacy…"

"You can give him grief all you want, but let's keep this visit between us, okay?" Tuck's smile is as sheepish as his posture. "Especially if you come to the charity ball. I don't want Zac to be more mad at me than he already is."

I eye him suspiciously before nodding my head in agreement. "I'll keep it a secret, for now."

The night air suddenly chills as I watch Tuck make his way back to his car. My skin is covered with goosebumps along the flesh of my arms, opposite hands flying up to rub my skin and generate some heat. I make a mental note to start the fire as soon as I go inside.

I'm about to turn around when Tuck calls out to me from his car. "Hey, you know you never said if you were still going to go with Zac to the charity ball?"

"No, I didn't, did I?" Looking at Tuck, a devilish grin takes over my features and a thrill rushes through my veins. "I guess you'll just have to wait and see."

With a flick of my wrist, I wave goodbye to Tuck and head back inside before he has a chance to retort. I still don't know if I'm going, mostly because I'm not sure what it'll mean if I do.

Will it mean I forgive Zac and I'm ready to try a date with him? Or will we just have a fun night together and that's it? Or do I stay home and we can all go back to how we were and pretend none of this ever happened?

Yeah. That last idea is terrible.

Closing the door behind me, I walk into the kitchen and reheat my dinner, only to start laughing. Zac and Tuck and their little bet. Boys may be boys, but these two boys seem to have learned a lesson.

Yes, don't mess with women is one part of this, but also... don't mess with me.

TWENTY-FOUR

Zac

"So, this is where she's supposed to meet you?"

Tuck stands next to me outside of the charity ball under the wisteria-draped entrance. Around us, people mill about, wandering in and out of the venue, which is an old historical hotel ballroom on the edge of Sweetkiss Creek. Couples walk arm in arm, smiling, and to be honest, it's kind of hurting my heart.

I've stood here for the last thirty minutes, waiting for Etta to arrive. I'd tried one last-ditch attempt earlier today to get ahold of her, but she still isn't answering my calls, so I texted her to let her know I'd be right here at the main door waiting for her if she still wanted to be my date.

I glance at my watch as Tuck shifts his weight from one foot to the other, shoving his hands in his pockets as he sighs and cranes his neck, looking around. "Are you sure she's coming?"

"No, I'm not sure. I asked her to meet me here at eight." My palms are slick and my mouth is dry. I flag down a server, requesting a glass of water. He promises to find me one and runs off as I wipe my hands on my suit.

"Eight?" Tuck's voice is incredulous as he rolls his eyes. "We've been out here since seven-fifteen."

I can feel my brother's gaze as he watches me. "I didn't want to not be out here when...if...no, *when* she shows up."

Tuck nods before he reaches into his jacket, pulling a small envelope out of it. A small familiar-looking envelope. In fact, if my eyes don't deceive me, it's the envelope which I know holds that stupid baseball card.

"I want to give you this." He thrusts the envelope in my direction.

I look at the envelope clutched in his grasp. "Why now? Don't you want to wait to see if she shows up before you part with your dear beloved card?"

"Don't throw it all back on me. I may have suggested the bet, but you took it." Taking my arm, he palms the envelope into my hand, squeezing it a few times before he wraps his arms around me and gives me a quick hug. "This card is yours. It's worth some money, you know, so...I don't know. Go crazy. Sell it and use the money to win back your woman—you can buy a lot of flower arrangements with the profits from selling that card to a collector."

Opening the envelope, I pull the baseball card out to look at it, flipping it over front to back. To think something this small could be worth so much money. Sliding it back into the envelope, I keep it clutched in my hand for the time being.

A quick look at my watch tells me it's almost eight. The entranceway, which was busy before with everyone arriving, has thinned out. There's even room for me to pace on the walkway now, so I do, as Tuck flicks a gaze toward the entrance.

"I'm gonna go inside. I'll see you at the table?"

His question feels like it's loaded with heavy artillery, and it's all aimed my way. Will he see me at the table? Will I come inside if she doesn't show up, or will I simply retreat and go home?

Will Etta even show up?

Taking a slow breath, I nod my head and attempt a carefree grin. "Of course. See you inside."

I watch Tuck as he makes his way through the entrance and disappears under the wisteria vines, headed for the ballroom. Looking around, I try to keep that carefree grin on my face as I fiddle with the envelope and wait for Etta. It's a good thing Tuck's left me alone since I need a few minutes to think things through—because he gave me an idea.

I'm determined to make this right, but the key ingredient needed for this apology recipe needs to be here first. So I pace some more.

The server who had taken my request for water ages ago is back. I take the glass of cold water he offers and down it in one go, handing it back to him with a flourish, and thanking him before he runs off.

More pacing. A quick look at my watch tells me it's now eight. I glance up and survey the parking lot, but there are no stragglers. There's no one walking toward me. The buoyancy of knowing what I want to do is still here, but it's waning. I don't want it to wane. I want to—

"Hey."

Spinning around, my heart slides into my throat when I find Etta standing in front of me wearing the most stunning off-the-shoulder gown I've ever seen. The most dangerous smile I've ever had the pleasure of being treated to dances on her lips.

"You're here." Yep. That's all I manage to eek out.

Still smiling, she takes a step toward me. "I'm here."

An electric shock rages across my body, and I can't move. Thank goodness I can speak.

"I'm glad you came." Looking out at the parking lot, I

laugh. "I've been standing here watching for your car to pull in."

"I came in through the entrance on the other side of the hotel. It's where the cab dropped me off." She takes a slow and careful step toward where I stand. "I feel like we should talk before we go inside."

Holding up a hand, I wave it in the air to stop her. "You're right, we do. But I want you to listen to me, okay?"

Etta's eyes narrow slightly as she puts a hand on her hip. "Okay. You have the floor."

My stomach turns a giant somersault as I hold up the envelope I've been clutching in my hand. My feet can finally move from where I'm rooted, so I step forward and place the envelope in her hand.

She looks at the envelope, then back at me. "What is this?"

"It is *the* card."

Recognition flickers in her eyes. "Ahhh. The baseball card. And what do you want me to do with it? Rip it up?"

"Oh, no, please don't do that." Chuckling, I take her other hand. Pulling it to my lips, I kiss it, allowing my mouth to linger on the back of her hand a little longer than intended. "This card is more yours than mine. I can't say I'm sorry in any more languages—"

"Saying it in Vulcan was a nice touch," Etta acknowledges, her mouth quirking at the corners.

"Glad you liked it." If I'm not reading things wrong, she seems to be more receptive to me, so I keep going. "Like I was saying, you've heard enough from me about this whole mess I created. Tuck gave me the card tonight to do what I want with. And what I want is to help you sell this card and use the money to put into your business."

Etta's eyes widen as she snaps her hand back from my grasp. "Say what?"

"I know you want to open that business and you can't

without funds. This card will give you plenty. Besides, it's the only way I can tell you how sorry I am. Again. And I'll keep telling you that as long as you'll allow me to because I don't want to be in a world that doesn't have Etta McCoy by my side, okay?"

Watching her face is like seeing a storm clear, in its own beautiful way. Watching her as she holds the envelope and flips it around in her hands, I can tell my words are sinking in.

But man, am I shocked when she hands that envelope right back to me.

"No."

"No?"

"Oh, sorry." Etta's hands fly to her hair as she smoothes it. "I should have said no, thank you."

"You don't want the card?" I feel like one of those giant balloons in the Macy's Thanksgiving Day Parade. Not the balloons at the start of the parade—the ones filled full to the brim with air. More like the balloons at the end of the parade, when they're deflated and lying lifeless on empty city streets.

"It's not that I don't want it, it's that I don't need it." Etta's expression is peaceful and her eyes are sparkling. "Steve is gone, there is no more lawsuit, and he has transferred the funds I needed to open the business into my bank account as of this morning. So, no. I don't need the baseball card."

"That was my hail Mary moment, you know," I manage sheepishly.

"It's generous of you to offer that, but you don't need a 'hail Mary' with me, Zac." Etta's eyes find mine as she stands on her tiptoes and kisses my cheek. "You're forgiven."

This woman. She is maddening, oh-so-baffling, and to boot, she's forgiving. Forgiving me and standing here, in front of me, showing up. It's at this moment I know for certain I am absolutely, unapologetically, one hundred percent head over heels for this woman.

Reaching out, I pull her closer, wanting to feel her in my arms. Etta threads her hands behind my neck as I lean down to rest the tip of my nose on hers. We breathe as one, our foreheads lightly touching.

Her fingers begin a little dance along my spine, causing a tremor across my flesh. Ever so slowly, I bring my mouth down and slant it across those amazingly luscious lips of hers. Her kiss tastes of jasmine and chewing gum, and the heady mixture is fast becoming my Kryptonite.

Her hand cups the back of my head, her fingers tugging on my hair. Gripping her waist, I pull her even tighter against me, never wanting this kiss to end. Not now, not tomorrow, not next week, not even in ten years' time. Never ever.

When we finally untangle ourselves, Etta tilts her head back, and everything inside of me turns into gooey mush. My hands can't stop moving along her arms, feeling the smoothness of her skin underneath my touch.

Pulling her close again, I nuzzle her neck.

"I'm in love with you," I murmur. It's my new hail Mary, because I do not want to lose this woman ever.

"Yeah?" Pulling back, Etta's head tilts to the side, and she purses her lips in thought.

I pull her back to me, laughing. "Yes. I love you, Etta. I love you, I love those dogs, and I love it when we argue."

Etta holds a finger in the air. "Debate. We don't argue, we debate."

"Fine," I say with a grin. "I love debating with you. Satisfied?"

She nods, resting her head on my shoulder and sighing.

"I love you, too."

The words are so softly spoken, I'm concerned I didn't hear her right. "Did you just say that you love me?"

Her cheeks go bright crimson, but there's no one around to see. "I do. And we know Thor loves you, so you just need to get Hercules on your side now. Canine companionship. It's a real thing, you know."

Laughing, I pull her close. "Oh, I know."

Suddenly I'm hit with a lightning bolt kind of thought. It's so good, I can't believe I didn't see it before. Seriously! Now, where did I put that envelope?

Stepping away from Etta, I shove my hand into my pockets, relieved when I find the card right back inside my jacket. It'll stay there for safekeeping for now.

"What are you doing?" she manages with a giggle.

"Making sure I have that baseball card, that's what I'm doing." I can't resist snaking my arm around her waist and pulling her tight to my body one more time. "We—you and me—are going to donate the funds from the sale of this card to the canine program."

Etta's eyes almost pop out of her head. "We...what?"

"This card will give us enough money to get the program off the ground and then some. And since you don't need the funds, then I can give it as a donation from us. But there will be a caveat."

"Caveat?" Cracking up, Etta's hands hold on to my elbows, her eyes pleading with me to go on. "What caveat could you have?"

"That they name the training grounds after your dogs. I'm thinking it's a power statement. 'Thercules Training Park.' It's got a nice ring to it, huh?"

Etta doubles over, laughing and wiping tears from her eyes. "You're kidding, right?"

"Not one bit, unless you want it to be the 'Thorcules Training Park'?" I laugh as she reaches out and takes my hand. "I'm never going to kid with you again. No bets, no jokes, no more getting arrested..."

"Shush." Etta's lips find mine and they do their job of

silencing me. Her hand caresses the side of my face, her thumb trailing a line along my jaw, and I fight an inward groan.

Slowly, she pulls her mouth from mine and tugs on my hand. "Come on," she says with a whisper, "let's go inside. You need to get that baseball card to Lane. This charity ball just became a party."

Nodding, I allow her to lead the way. Only, as we're about to go back inside, I stop her once more. "Wait."

Etta turns around, looking a touch impatient. "What now?"

"I don't just love you, you know. I am in love with you. It's deep. I'm in a freefall and it's amazing. You're amazing." My eyes bounce back and forth with hers, wanting...no, needing her to truly hear me. "I plan to never let you go. Got it?"

"Well, look at that. We agree for once," Etta says as she takes one step back toward me and falls, giggling, into my arms. "I'm yours. Always."

I kiss her forehead one more time as we're both pulled closer, like magnets. Etta McCoy. Not only is she the fire to my ice, she's also the yin to my yang.

As she drops her head back onto my shoulder, I wrap my arms tighter around her. I can feel the rise and fall of her breath as she nuzzles herself even closer.

I hope this moment never ends.

Epilogue
ETTA

Pulling up outside the police station, I slow my car to a stop and put the gear into park. I have a list as long as my leg to get done today, and Thor choosing this very Saturday morning to pull his runaway-doggy trick is not on there.

But I can't get mad at the fact he's here with Zac. So, it's out of my way? I'll just sneak in a few kisses before I leave with the little critter.

Pushing open the heavy door on the old building, I'm surprised the lobby area isn't bustling like it usually is. There doesn't seem to be an officer or anyone stationed at the front today, so I peer over to the shared open space beyond. My hand flies in the air as soon as I spot Kenny, the guy who shares a desk with Zac. I wave him over, grateful when he obliges.

"You here for the escape artist?" Kenny grins as he crosses the room to meet me.

"Guilty, officer." I look around the room again, still surprised that I've only seen Kenny since I got here. "Is Zac here?"

Kenny nods his head as he points to the back area where the cells are. "You'll find him that way."

As I make my way across the room, I stop once to glance back at Kenny. It's super weird to find him grinning when I do.

A few more steps and I'm crossing the threshold into the jail cells, an area I'm sadly all too familiar with thanks to my boyfriend. It's fine though. I'll get him back one day, that's for sure.

"Zac? Hello?" My voice echoes in the small space. It's darker here than I remember. "You here?"

"Hey, back here, in the last cell."

I know the cell only too well. "Ah, the cell you put me in when you arrested me?"

Chuckling, Zac pops his head around the corner and waves. "Come on. I've got Thor."

"I'm coming, but no silver bracelets today, okay?"

He smiles that smile at me, the one that makes my tummy flip and sends a thousand fluttery feathers across my skin.

He holds up his hands for me to see they're empty. "No bracelets. Just Thor."

"Sorry about this. I swear, that dog is in love with you." Shaking my head, I follow Zac inside the lockup area...only to stop in my tracks when I enter. My hand flies to my mouth, my eyes darting around the small cell. "What have you done?"

As the words come out of my mouth, in an instant we're surrounded by light. The ceiling is layered with twinkling fairy lights of white, and Zac is hopping around the tiny space trying to light some candles. What looks like a bucket of ice is sitting on the bench with two glasses.

Sitting on the floor, next to a pile of—baseball cards?—is Thor, looking really guilty as he eats a rawhide treat.

Putting one hand on my hip, I keep my eyes trained on

Thor. "Are you keeping rawhides at the station now to give to runaway dogs?"

Hands find my waist as Zac comes up behind me, leaning his body into mine and wrapping his arms around my middle. My body melts into his as I lean into him, inhaling his scent as I lean the back of my head on his shoulder. Soft kisses land on the top of my head, and I close my eyes and sigh.

"That was an enormous sigh," Zac says, his voice low and husky.

"It's a content one," I manage, turning my body around oh-so-slowly so I can face him. Zac takes the cue, and folds me into his embrace, his thumb and forefinger caressing my chin as his lips lightly brush against mine.

He pulls away, and I jokingly pull him back. "I'm not content with that."

"Okay, I see how this is gonna be, McCoy." Zac threads his fingers through my hair with one hand while the other one steadies me on my lower back. I'm in sensory overload as his lips slant across mine. This kiss is the most perfect kiss I've ever had. It's uncomplicated and real. It's full of promise and sprinkled with forever. Clutching his uniform, I tug him closer, feeling every inch of him shudder when I do.

I can feel my body temperature rising on this cool fall day. I'd thrown an old sweatshirt on when I ran out of the house and I was wishing at this moment it was a tank top. This kiss is that good.

His lips are soft, warm, and dangerous...I could stay here all day. I pull away, taking a breath and let Zac's fingertips trace invisible lines from the top of my head, down my neck and arms until he's holding both of my hands in his, kissing them.

Still holding my hands, he takes a step back. "You know how much I love you, don't you?"

"Of course I do," I manage as I feel heat rise to my cheeks. "I love you, too."

"Good." Letting go of my hands, he points to the pile of baseball cards on the floor. "There's something in there for you."

"The last time there was a baseball card involved—"

"Lesson learned," he laughs. "Come on. Trust me?"

Of course I trust him, but that doesn't stop me from shooting him a look as I crouch down and rifle through the cards. "What am I looking for, anyway? A Cal Ripken card?"

"Just move them around." Zac crosses his arms, cocking his head to one side and holding up his arm to show me his watch. "I'm timing you."

"If you're trying to instill fear in me, it's working," I giggle, my hands sorting through the cards, still unsure what I'm looking for...until I find it.

When I pick up one of his precious baseball cards, I notice its weight. I drag my eyes to his, but he's busy petting Thor suddenly, not giving anything away.

I turn my attention back to the card. As I flip it over, my jaw hits the floor.

Secured by a few strips of scotch tape is the most beautiful engagement ring I've ever seen.

"Zac?" My eyes slam into his and he grins.

Ever so slowly, he lowers to the floor onto one knee, Thor laying down beside him as he does, as if he planned it this way.

"What do you say, Etta? Will you spend forever with me?"

My breath hitches and in a moment, a life with Zac flashes in front of my eyes. It's full of laughter and love; there's family and friends, but lots of dogs, too. There's Christmas and New Year, and all the holidays rolled up into one like a perfect dessert—you know the kind, it has lots of extra icing piled high with a sweetness that can go on for days.

And there's Zac. My Zac. In every way, each step. My forever love.

Leaning down, I touch my forehead to his as I kiss the tip

of his nose. "I don't think I can have it any other way. Yes, Zac Wright, I'll spend forever with you no matter how long that is."

With a whoop of happiness, Zac jumps up and puts the ring on my finger, yelling out as he does. "It's safe. You all can come out now she said yes!"

As a cheer erupts outside of the cells, I look at Zac, my eyes widening as all the lights come back on. "Were all of your co-workers here this whole time?"

He throws his head back and laughs. "Didn't you wonder why a police station was so quiet?"

"Wow." I step back, looking down at my hand and at the ring, its facets hitting the light and sparkling like a thousand tiny diamonds. "You must really love me then, huh?"

I don't need an answer. His lips across mine tell me everything.

Thank you so much for reading The Art of Falling in Love with Your Enemy!

Amelia and Spencer's story is coming in November, right in time for **Christmas** - and I'm REALLY thrilled to be writing this book.

Let's just say it is loosely based on a true life story... and yes, I had to ask permission share it!

If you want to stay up to date on this release (and other ones too!), you can do it by signing up for my newsletter here.

If you're looking for more content like *bonus scenes*, *surprise chapters*, and *swag*, or maybe you want to have **early access** to Amelia and Spencer's book BEFORE it's released, then come and join me on Ream! It's a subscription service, like Netflix but waaaay more affordable and interactive, where

I can give you even more stories ***and*** you get voting power on some of my covers, characters for books, and so much more!

Happy reading!

Anne xo

Also by Anne Kemp

Sweetkiss Creek Series

Welcome to Sweetkiss Creek, where the locals are nosy, the dogs are pushy, and love could be just around the corner...

The Sweetkiss Creek series are closed door rom coms, filled with close friendships, swoony kisses, and lots of laughs!

The Art of Falling in Love with Your Best Friend

Dylan and Reid's story

The Art of Falling in Love with Your Enemy

Etta and Zac's story-thank you for reading!

The Art of Falling in Love...Again

Amelia and Spencer's story

Coming November '23

The Art of Falling in Love with Your Grumpy Boss

Riley and Brett's story

TBD early '24

Love in Lake Lorelei Series

Ahhh...Lake Lorelei, the small town down the road from Sweetkiss Creek. These sweet romcoms are sizzling with chemistry and bringing you all the feels.

Get to know this small town, its locals and, most importantly, the Lake Lorelei Fire Department!

Sweet Summer Nights (Book 1)

Freya and Wyatt's story

The Sweet Spot (Book 2)

Ari and Carter's story

When Sparks Fly (Book 3)

Maisey and Jack's story

The Abby George Series

The Abby George books are closed-door, Chick lit comedies with a lil' sass, a touch of sarcasm, and some innuendo and language (especially from the salty captain!) but guaranteed to have you laughing out loud as you fall in love!

Rum Punch Regrets

Gotta Go To Come Back

Sugar City Secrets

Caribbean Romance Novella

Part of the Abby George world but can be read as a stand alone story.

This book is a sweet and clean closed door

romantic comedy.

Second Chance for Christmas

Stay up-to-date on new releases, get special bonus content, and special promotions when you sign up for

Anne's newsletter.

Acknowledgments

With each book, new amazing people move to my 'village' - or into my world. These are people who I've met somehow, usually in a bookish manner. We may have met on social media or through my newsletter, or through a writing event or at an authors' conference.

I am not sure how I meet them, it just matters that they're here. :) If you're one of those people and you're seeing this note - thank you for being here. I'm glad you are!

Working on this book, I hit some personal challenges. I honestly didn't know if I would finish this book or if I had the energy to...but lucky for me, I have an amazing support team behind me who kept me going. These folks (readers, fellow authors, and family) gave me energy when I needed it - you know who you are - and I hope one day to repay them or to at least be here when they need me.

Because it takes a village.

To my editor Sara Kingsley....without your input, feedback, patience, and guidance this wouldn't be the book it is. THANK YOU.

Thank you to my assistant Sabrina Rivera for helping clear items off my plate so I could write this book. You're a rockstar!

For Glen, the patient husband: thank you for keeping things running semi-smoothly (ha!) when I disappear for hours and days to push my book babies over the line. Your support keeps me going.

And to you, the reader who may be skimming this right

now--thank you for picking up my book and reading it. I hope you enjoyed the story.

To all of the lovers and dreamers out there, don't ever stop loving and dreaming. This world needs you.

Anne xo

About Anne

Anne Kemp is an author of romantic comedies, sweet contemporary romance, and chick lit.
She loves reading (and does it ridiculously fast, too!), gluten-free baking
(because everyone needs a hobby that makes them crazy), and finding time to binge-watch her favorite shows. She grew up in Maryland but made Los Angeles her home until she encountered her own real-life meet-cute at a friend's wedding where she ended up married to one of the groomsmen.
For real.

Anne now lives on the Kapiti Coast in New Zealand, and even though she was married at Mt. Doom, no...she doesn't have a Hobbit. However, she and her husband do have a terrier named George Clooney and a rescue pup named Charlie. When she's not writing, she's usually with them taking a long walk on the river by their home.

www.annekemp.com

www.ingramcontent.com/pod-product-compliance
Lightning Source LLC
Chambersburg PA
CBHW022056290426
44109CB00014B/1126